Twisted Yarns

Twisted Yarns

Written and researched by: *Su Barton and Rhianydd Murray*

With contributions by: *Bill Partridge and Mel Read*

Published by: *North Warwickshire & Hinckley College*

Designed by: *Samantha Curtis*

Printed by: *The Print Studio Ltd, Leicester*

Acknowledgements:
Bill Boggon, Cynthia Brown, Peter Hewis, Prof. Pierre Lanfranchi, Leicestershire Records Office, Phillip Lindley, Ted Murray, Rosemary Shaller, Prof. Wray Vamplew.

Thanks to:
Various people for their help and advice in the writing of 'Factory Life' and 'Social Life in the Factory' and all the people who volunteered to discuss and write about their personal experiences.

Contents

Foreword

By Mel Read,
Labour Member of the European Parliament for Nottingham and Leicestershire N.W.

Yarns about yarn are woven into our history. References are in both old and new testaments, in Shakespeare and Chaucer, in the gory knitting of those watching the guillotine in the French Revolution and in Jane Austin. More recently, the fashion industry, one of Britain's major exports, permeates soap operas and TV comedies.

For over 350 years, thousands of people in Hinckley have worked in the textile industry. As the millenium nears, fewer and fewer people depend on this kind of work. Yet in so many ways, it has made a major contribution to what Hinckley and the surrounding area are today.

Twisted Yarns is the story of these people. Describing itself as "the yarns of the past weaving the future", or in the case of Hinckley "knitting the future", the book and the project on which it is based examines the cultural heritage of the textile industry in this part of Leicestershire.

Funded by the European Union, this book is part of a larger project, with similar work being undertaken on the textile industries of Portugal, Spain, Ireland and France.

In many ways, it is a landmark project, and was recently judged by the European Commission as one of the most innovative around. While so many EU projects are rightly concerned with modern day requirements of employment and training, there is nevertheless, a place for reminding ourselves and others of our heritage.

The Yarns of the Past Weaving the Future

EVIDENCE OF THE EARLY INDUSTRY IN HINCKLEY

People in the Hinckley knitting community are proud of the fact that their town, although not the place of its invention, was the first town in Leicestershire, if not the East Midlands, to be producing machine made stockings commercially. Traditionally this was thanks to William Illiffe who was working a framework knitting machine, which he had bought for £60, in Hinckley by 1640 at least 40 years before the trade began in Leicester. This is according to Nichols (1) who wrote his History of Hinckley several generations later in 1782. Whilst the claims for Illiffe, who was Nichol's wife's ancestor, cannot be proven documentarily, he could have had the oral reminiscences of older members of his wife's family on which to base his assertion. As we shall see later in this book, oral history can be used to fill the gaps left by documentary history. Without any evidence to the contrary, there is no reason not to believe that William Iliffe brought the first knitting frame to Leicestershire. Knitting may have been an attractive trade to get into as, in 1260 when the town was part of Simon de Montfort's lands, Hinckley had been declared a town where strangers might buy or sell wool without a fine. Both A J Pickering (2) and H J Francis (3) in their excellent histories repeat the story told by Nichols but they do not claim to have found any new evidence. Pickering wrote that the actual place where William Iliffe worked on his frame is not known, although a few generations later, in 1693, another William Iliffe surrendered a lease of 1684 for the Bulls Head Inn, some barns and other buildings in an area known as Roundhill which was between the present Market Place and the Borough. Again in 1714 according to records of the Feoffees, the body responsible for pre-enclosure property in Hinckley, William Iliffe the elder, together with John Foster were granted a lease for property, again in the Roundhill area which included the town hall, a drapery and a butchery (4). These people were not necessarily direct descendants of the original William. Pickering also shows us that the Iliffes were established in Hinckley at least by 1585. The parish registers for that year record that an Iliffe (spelled Ilive) married Alicia Wright (5).

This section of the book shows what can be discovered about a place and a particular group of people through an investigation using just a few old

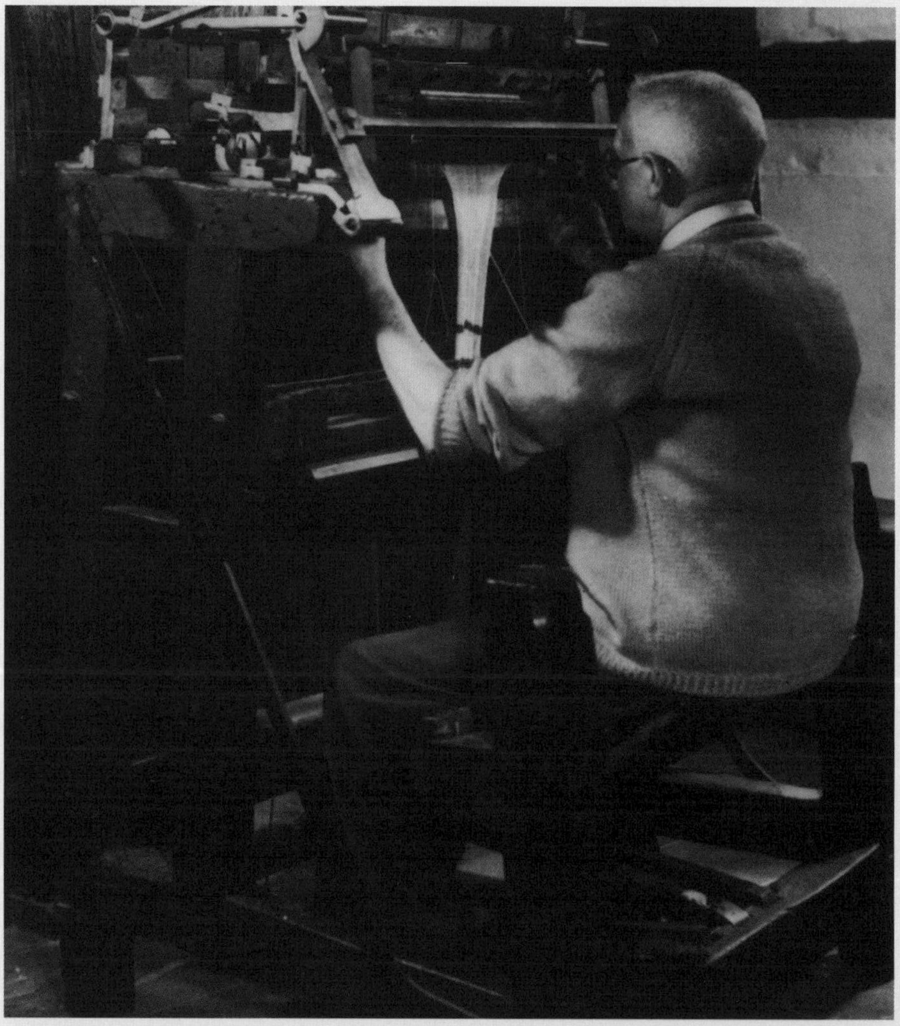

A framework knitter demonstrates using the knitting frame in Hinckley Museum, reputed to be the oldest.

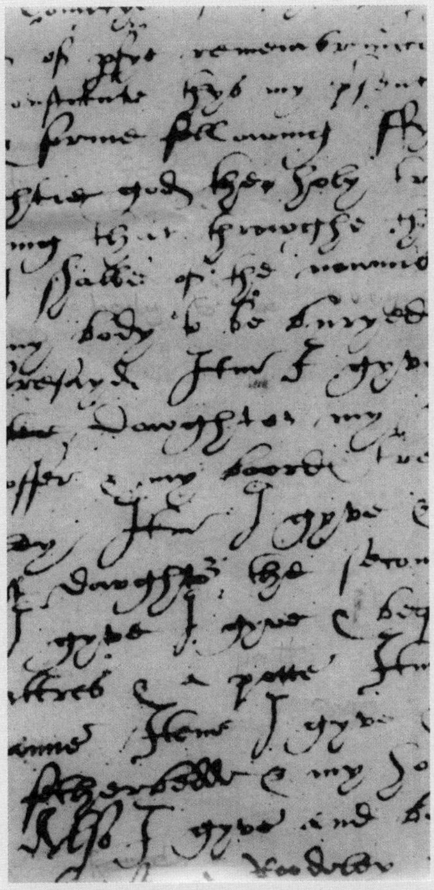

Part of the will of James Ylive (Illiffe), Hinckley 1558

documents. For the earlier history of the community this is all the written evidence that remains but it is possible to piece together a sketchy image of the people of the times. The real evidence of their lives is the knitting community they helped to establish in the town.

It can be proved that a family with the name of Iliffe lived in Hinckley even earlier than Pickering found. A will of James Iliffe (this time it appears to be spelled Ylive), dated 1558 can be seen in Leicestershire Records Office. James Iliffe, like his later relatives was a man in trade. He was a tailor who had enough property to make leaving a will a necessity. He may not have been a direct ancester of William Iliffe's as James seems to have had daughters not sons to carry on the family name, but he could have been the brother or cousin of an ancestor. What James Iliffe's will tells us is that members of the Iliffe family were established in Hinckley by the early to mid sixteenth century as James was an adult in 1558 with seemingly grown-up children. The will also shows us that he was in trade and therefore not wholly dependent on agriculture for the means of subsistence. He worked in a textile based occupation, tailoring, and lived at least comfortably for the times, not living at subsistence level as the majority of peasants would have done in those days. As trade grew and living standards improved through the Elizabethan and early Stuart period, this is the kind of family which a couple of generations later might have been in a position to risk investing £60 on a contraption whose financial viability in local market conditions was at the time unproven.

It cannot be proved, as Pickering found, where William Iliffe's knitting frame was worked. Using new evidence not found by Pickering, it can be shown that some members of the Iliffe family held hereditary property rights in a part of Hinckley known as Castle End, at the top of the present day Castle Street. During the preparations for the wedding of William Iliffe's grandson, John, to Christian Robinson, an agreement regarding the sale and lease of the Castle End premises was drawn up which provided a home for the couple. In it John is described as a framework knitter, as are the other Castle End inhabitants. John was already living in Castle End with or near his mother, Hannah, the widow of William Iliffe's son Joseph, who in 1715, the year of the indenture, had been dead for twenty years. Hannah had since been remarried to John Woodward, another framework knitter and they too lived at Castle End. Another member of the little group was George Wood the elder, yet another framework knitter. George Wood was presumably the father of Hannah as her maiden name had been Wood. Each member of the family had legal rights of occupancy which had to be taken into account when John married. George Wood, John Woodward and his wife Hannah and John Iliffe were all parties to the complicated legal document which transferred ownership to Thomas Sansome, yeoman, and George Wood the younger, yet another framework knitter. The original parchment document can be seen in Leicestershire Records Office. John Iliffe received £60 from Thomas Robinson, his prospective father-in-law, as Christian's marriage portion. In pre-enclosure Hinckley, that is before 1760, the lords of the manor according to the Enclosure Act were Thomas Sansome and Joseph Robinson. This may explain Sansome's involvement in what was otherwise a family transaction. The agreement to the sale and subsequent transfer of the lease also refers to members of the Robinson family having occupied the land at an unspecified time in the past, prior to the then occupiers of the messuage, either the Wood or the Iliffe family. George Wood the elder and John Woodward were given 5 shillings

---

1 *Nichols, History and Curiosities of Hinckley, 1782*

2 *A J Pickering, The Cradle and Home of the Hosiery Trade, Hinckley, 1945*

3 *H J Francis, History or Hinckley, Hinckley, 1930*

4 *Pickering, p20*

5 *Pickering, p18-19.*

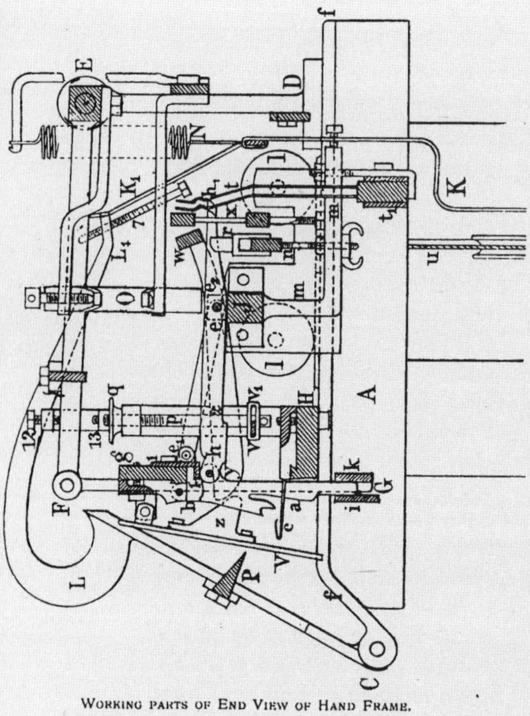

WORKING PARTS OF END VIEW OF HAND FRAME.

Diagram showing the complexity of the handframe, from 'The Hand Knitting Frame' by Quilter and Chamberlain, 1912. Published by the freinds of Wigston Framework Knitters Museum, 1992

each by Sansome and Wood the younger. The property's ownership was to be transferred to the new owners on the marriage of John and Christian who were to occupy a piece of the Castle End messuage or cottage, terms which referred to a piece of land and the buildings upon it. A messuage or cottage would have been unlikely to have enough land around it or confer the right of use of enough strips in the common and open fields of unenclosed Hinckley to provide an adequate living for the occupants and so they would have had to supplement production from their own land by working on someone else's who had a larger area. The Iliffes, Woods and Woodwards enhanced their household income by framework knitting. To the east the messuage was bordered by Palmer's Lane. All the parties were to have access to and from their own homes and land across the property and each was to be allowed to "hang and dry his clothes there". The area apportioned for the use of John and Christian was for the rest of their natural lives: after the decease of the longer lived of them it was designated to be for the use of their joint heirs forever. All the occupants were to remain living on Castle End. In a seemingly strange arrangement Wood the elder, John and Hannah Woodward and John Iliffe were to continue living there virtually rent free. They were to pay rent of one peppercorn on 25 March. This arrangement applied not just to the persons living at the time but also to their heirs (6). As Wood seems to have been his maternal grandfather and the Woodwards were his mother and step-father, this arrangement seems to have conveyed the future lease of the property to John Iliffe and his heirs, with George Wood the younger, probably John's uncle and his descendants jointly with those of Thomas Sansome, owning the land.

This family of framework knitters were all closely connected with the original William Iliffe who seems to have established through his influence a community of framework knitters, as his son, grandson, son's father-in-law and grandson's step-father are all described as such. From the documents it is not possible to tell whether the messuage at Castle End was the marital home of Joseph and Hannah whose father had come to live with her and which she retained during her widowhood as a home for their son. If so, it is possible that they inherited the lease from William and it could also explain the complicated arrangements regarding the lease which safeguarded John and Christian's right to a family home even after the sale of the property. George Wood the younger, one of the purchasers, did not live there, which implies the Wood family home was elsewhere, perhaps the home his father had left to live with Hannah. It would also explain why they only received 5 shillings compensation for the sale of the property. Alternatively, the Wood family might have occupied the land, the younger George having set up a home elsewhere. This arrangement might have been a means for George the elder to provide for his daughter and grandson, John, while ostensibly still leaving the property to his own son. This idea is supported by reference in the document to John Wood, occupier of premises once purchased from a Mr Sands, adjacent to the plot allocated to John and Christian. If this supposition is true it leaves a mystery as to what happened to the first William Illiffe's property after his death. If he had been as successful a framework knitter as historians of the industry imply, then he must have had at least a home as well as his stocking frame to leave to his son, Joseph. After all, he had been respectable enough to marry the daughter of a clergyman, Elizabeth Cleveland, sister of the well-

6 *These agreements are contained in two documents of Lease and Release held in Leicestershire Records Office, reference DE4511/129/2. Lease and release was a procedure for transferring land from one party to another without the necessity of enrolment. The intending new owner first took a lease of the property for one year, which could be done by a deed that did not need to be enrolled. Then, a day later, in this case the day of John and Christian Iliffe's marriage, the vendor conveyed the lease to the purchaser, that, being only a right could be transferred without enrolment on a court roll, since possession did not pass as a result. This procedure was a way of taking advantage of a loophole in the Statute of Uses of 1535-36 and allowed private or secret conveyance of property or for it to be left to a person other than the eldest son. (Definition taken from Terrick V H Fitzhugh, The Dictionary of Genealogy, London, 1988 edition).*

known poet John. If he had been unable to make a reasonable living framework knitting his neighbours would not have wanted to emulate him by purchasing their own frames to enter the trade themselves. Another possibility is that Joseph or, after his death, his widow, did not prosper in the trade and were forced to give up their home and move in with Hannah's family.

Six years after John died in 1742 , Christian took out a lease for a messuage in the Borough where her second son George, an inn holder, took on adjacent premises in 1753 (6). Perhaps her eldest son Joseph continued to live at Castle End. The valuation of houses and appurtenances of Hinckley made in January 1782 shows that Joseph Iliff was quite a prosperous man, leasing from the Great Feoffment a house worth £1.15shillings, owning two others valued at £1.10 each, occupied by Charles Challoner and Samuel Wickes, whilst himself living in a house with garden valued at £9. 10 shillings. The valuation, unfortunately, does not give the location of these properties.

Another member of the Iliffe family, Edward, was also living at Castle End at around that time. What his relationship to John was is so far undiscovered. When he died in 1758 he left a wife, Esther and three sons called Joseph, James and William, typical Iliffe family names, and a daughter, Sarah. The will of Edward Iliffe, also a framework knitter, bequeathed a messuage of land at Castle End to his wife Esther for her lifetime and then to his sons, Joseph, James and William. His property included "one frame engine for the making of hose". His daughter, Sarah Smith, who had married a Hereford man called Robert Smith received along with each of her brothers £5. Castle End must have been quite a bustling and crowded part of the town with so many framework knitters working and living in the same small area. In 1715 there were other occupants there, as a neighbour of the Wood, Woodward and Iliffe family, named as Thomas Boonham, lived in property to the west, formerly occupied by William Shenton. Other neighbours of the family in Castle End were John and Thomas Newton, also framework knitters, John's wife Katherine living on messuages known as Newton's Yard and Samuel Isard a frame-smith; they were all living there in 1728 (7). Later that century, in 1792, Thomas Needham was also working in Castle End in the closely related trade of dyer and trimmer.

Knitting Frame owned by H Flude and Co, Hinckley.
'One frame engine for the making of Hose'

6 *Pickering, p20*

7 *Lease and Release Deed, 24 and 25 October 1728, LRO DE 451/131/1-2*

Interestingly, in 1763 the founder of the Catholic Church in Hinckley, Father Norton, obtained the services of Joseph Iliff, a hosier, who negotiated the purchase of a house and land on the outskirts of the town at the top end of Castle Street (8), probably part of the Castle End message. The lack of a final letter E to the name Iliff, as related here by Pickering, seems to indicate that the Joseph who helped establish the Roman Catholic Church in Hinckley was the son of John and Christian. Pickering wrote that Joseph dropped the E from his name. His Wood family ancestors, the owners of the land, are remembered in the present day Wood Street.

A young widow called Anne, whose husband William Iliffe (obviously not the one who bought the first stocking frame) had died only a year earlier than she did in 1723 at the age of about 32, left a will in 1724. The entry in the register recording her burial describes her as being about 30 years old. A search of the register though shows that Anne Cooper, daughter of Robert Cooper who later married a William Iliffe, was born in 1691, so actually she was about 33 at the time of her death. She left all her property to her little boy, Robert, who was about 8 years old at the time, in trust during his minority under the care of his paternal grandfather, yet another William. Anne's other two children, Anne and Edward, had both died within six months of each other in December 1716 and May 1717. Anne at the age of 6 when Robert was 10 months old and Edward at the age of two when Robert was just five months old. It can be deduced from the inventory of Anne Iliffe's goods that the family were in trade of some sort.

A connection between them and the developing hosiery industry is through a witness to her will, Garrett Venable (sometimes with an S at the end). He lived for many years after the death of his friends, Anne and William. The John and William Venables who appear in the local Poll Book having voted in 1719 were probably the father and uncle or grandfather of Garrett who named two of his sons after them. Garrett was the only Venables voting by 1741. By 1753 Garrett had also passed away, leaving a widow, Sarah, and four little boys, John, William, James and Samuel. Sarah, his widow, was planning to remarry in 1753 and to protect the interests of her existing children a legal agreement was made between her, her proposed husband, some trustees and her children. This document describes Sarah as the widow and executrix of Garrett Venable, framework knitter. The agreement formed a settlement on her intended marriage to John Calow, another knitter. With Calow's consent, Sarah transferred to the use of the trustees, Joseph Robinson, yeoman and John Dalby, the schoolmaster, the property and effects of Garrett Venables to be held in trust for her children. This was on condition that Sarah enjoy the rents and issues of the property and the use of personal effects during her life. The property mentioned was four messages in the Bond End of Hinckley, at that time occupied by Sarah herself, Peter Ingram, Nathaniel Allsop and William Venable, possibly a brother-in-law. Also involved in this transaction were two "fframes (sic) or engines for making hose" as well as the personal and household goods of her late husband. The knitting frames were ultimately to be given to her son, Samuel, who appears to have been the youngest. This evidence shows the importance attached not just to real estate property but also to capital in the form of knitting frames. What happened to the younger generation of the Venables family is undiscovered, the name does not appear in the 1775 Poll Book. Perhaps they no longer owned sufficient property to allow any of them to vote. The Venable family, although the father was described as a framework knitter, obviously lived off rents from their property and probably also their knitting frames, as they owned more than one. They were also connected, either through business or friendship, with William and Anne Iliffe, making the unspecified trade of the Iliffe's shop likely to be connected with hosiery.

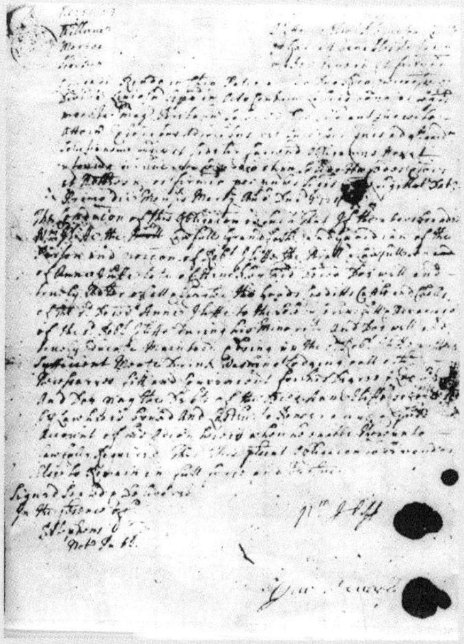

Will of Anne Iliffe, 1724

8 Pickering, p20

Wherever this Iliffe family lived might also be a contender as the site of the first stocking frame in Hinckley. Although Pickering believed that the original William Iliffe had three sons named after him, they had all died in infancy. Even so, it is highly likely that he had a brother, uncle or cousin who named a child after his much respected relative. Again the parish registers give evidence that this was the normal practice in the Iliffe and many other families at the time. William Iliffe, the husband of Anne was named after his father. William and Anne's three children were all named after family members, Edward was named after his uncle, Anne, after her mother and Robert, the only survivor past childhood, after his paternal grandfather. The family home of this branch of the family could have been the family home of the original William, the family sharing common ancestors as the same baptismal names persist over generations in different branches of the family. The inventory associated with her will, itemising Anne's property, shows that she was part of a family in trade. The most valuable item on the inventory is "goods in the shop", appraised to a total of £212.10s 4d. She also had £120 owing to her, possibly from business transactions. Curiously, her more personal property did not belong to her solely. Four books, a silver cup and silver buckles and buttons for a coat or waistcoat are valued at her half share. All her household goods had been sold at a public sale for £26, again hers was a half share of £13. Neither her will nor the inventory mention any other person who might be the joint owner of her personal property, perhaps she had inherited them jointly with a sister from her own parents, not her Iliffe husband. The parish register shows that other daughters were born to Robert Cooper, one of which was called Hannah.

A connection with this branch of the Iliffe family and the Iliffe's in Castle End is through the Cooper family. The widow Anne's maiden name was Cooper. A hosier called John Cooper, in 1753, was a witness to a lease for premises in the Borough, signed by George, the inn holder son of John and Christian, a great grandson of the first William (9). Even if they are not exactly the same family they were probably close blood relatives.

What ultimately became of the young orphan Robert has not yet been discovered but he voted in the election of 1741 as the Poll Book for that year shows. An entry in the parish registers for 1741 shows that he married Mary Adkins (or Atkins as Pickering writes it), maybe linking with another Hinckley hosiery family dynasty. Any relationship with the Atkins, the hosier family, has not been established and any connection between the families is purely speculation. Robert and Mary are not mentioned again in the parish registers. Pickering gives other information about the Iliffe's of Hinckley which can be viewed by anyone wishing to know more about the reputed first family "in the hosiery" in the town.

A search of the Hinckley Parish Registers shows the burial in 1725 of the first person to be listed in the register as a "fframework"(sic) knitter when a new volume began to sometimes give occupations. John Fisher was recorded as being over 80 at the time of his death. If his age was accurately recorded, John Fisher may have been one of the first time-served framework knitters in Leicestershire, entering the trade in the 1650's. The original William Iliffe was, according to Nichols, able to make a living from his frame by working it day and night with the help of an apprentice, the beginnings of shift working in the trade. Unless Iliffe's innovative use of technology in the town had been copied by his neighbours by the 1650s, John Fisher may even have worked or learned his trade on Iliffe's machine. John was fortunate as he lived into an old age shared by his wife, Lucy, who was buried only 2 days later than her husband on 7 April 1725, again her age is given as over 80. However, their ages may not have been known, only guessed at by the person entering the record in the register. Someone called John Fisher had been baptised in 1656, which if it were the same person would make him only 69 or 70 years old at the time of his death. We know from the example of the younger

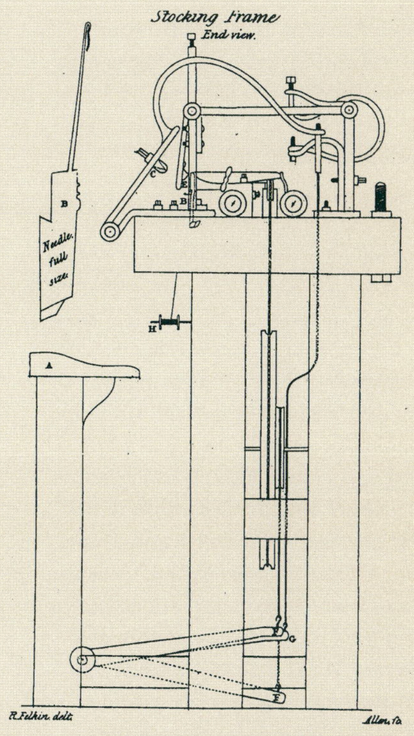

Diagram taken from W Felkin's "Account of the machine - Wrought Hosiery Trade" 1845.

William Iliffe and his wife, Anne, that these remarks relating to age were not always accurate.

Two other framework knitters are recorded as having been buried in 1725, the first year of the new register, giving some occupations. They were Nathaniel Wills who was aged about 30 in April 1725 and Jonas Kind, also about 30 years old, who was buried in November. Before this year it is not possible to identify the occupation or status of an individual using the Parish Records alone. We have to cross-reference to wills, deeds and indentures to find out more about the people in the registers.

Within 30 years, improvements to the basic frame as used by Iliffe were already being made. A Hinckley man called Needham made some additions to the basic frame in 1670 that were widely adopted (10).

Another early Hinckley hosier was Samuel Ward who left property valued at £251. 7s 9d in 1689. The inventory of his goods includes 3 spinning wheels, 3 bags of dying stuff, a twisting mill and implements in his "combe shoppe". He also left 241lb of yarn and 101 dozen and 6 pairs of hose valued at £29.7 shillings. He also had £95 owing to him, possibly from business transactions. No mention of a knitting frame is made so he does not seem to have made the hose himself. From the evidence of this inventory it can be seen that Samuel Ward probably put out yarn to stockingers who made it up on frames in their own cottages and brought the finished articles back to Ward to be sold. A witness to the inventory of Ward's property, which can be seen in Leicestershire Records Office, was a William Hurst, a member of another hosier family whose descendants would continue in the trade up to the present century. In 1782, Christopher Iliff, a stockinger only 17 years old married Sarah Hurst with the consent of his father William, linking the two families. Like the Iliffes, the Wards and Hursts were old established Hinckley families. A James Hurst was buried in 1565 according to the parish registers, and a person named Warde was also mentioned in 1562. The name Needham, referred to above, is also mentioned in an entry in 1562. These entries are on the first pages of the register.

All this speculation about individuals is interesting but not crucial to our understanding of the development of the hosiery trade in the Hinckley area. What is important to know about the Hinckley community is this. By the mid 1600's, over a century before the enclosure of the town's open fields and commons and before the time many people consider the industrial revolution to have properly started, framework knitting was already established not just in the town but in other Leicestershire villages. Looking at property left by framework knitters and hosiers in inventories attached to wills, we can see from items like cheese making equipment, that other more traditionally agrarian pursuits were still carried on in these hosier and stockinger households. An indenture of 1688 mentions one of the parties as a "silke stocken frame worke knitter in Hinckley", proving that even within the very early trade there was diversification and that not all the stockings made in the town were of the coarser woollen variety (11). Hinckley very soon specialised in making cotton hose. From all the evidence cited above, we know that within 60 years of the first framework knitting machine coming to Hinckley the trade was widespread within the vicinity.

10 Pickering
11 Pickering, p87

ENCLOSURE AND ITS EFFECTS

In the first century of framework knitting in Hinckley it was not, for many households involved in the trade, a full-time or primary occupation. In pre-enclosure Hinckley all established members of the community shared in the agricultural land surrounding the town. The cultivated land around the township was made up of very large open fields, divided up into strips of land which were shared between each household with rights to use them. This shared system was not a model of an egalitarian paradise. Some people had more rights to more or better land and therefore to potential wealth than others. The right to keep animals such as a cow, pigs or sheep on the common and the land attached to cottages meant that even the poorest could provide themselves with some food. Smaller land holders and those with little or no rights in the open fields could sell their labour to the more affluent with access to more land or, as happened in Hinckley, take up a productive occupation like framework knitting which could be carried out in the worker's own home. Some of the better-off townspeople might have provided wool and later silk and cotton for stockingers to work with, paying them a price for the knitting and seaming of the finished product. In this way some of the better off people became hosiers, like the Iliffes, Wards and Hursts, putting out work to poorer neighbours, as well as perhaps knitting for themselves, employing apprentices and organising the sale of the finished stockings to larger merchants. The poorer people became stockingers engaged in a cottage industry and later wage labourers.

In the agricultural township of unenclosed Hinckley, farm buildings were not scattered around the countryside as they are today. The open fields, that were feudal in origin and dated from the early medieval period, were not populated by farmhouses. All the farm buildings, houses, barns, stables and animal sheds were close together in the town itself (12).

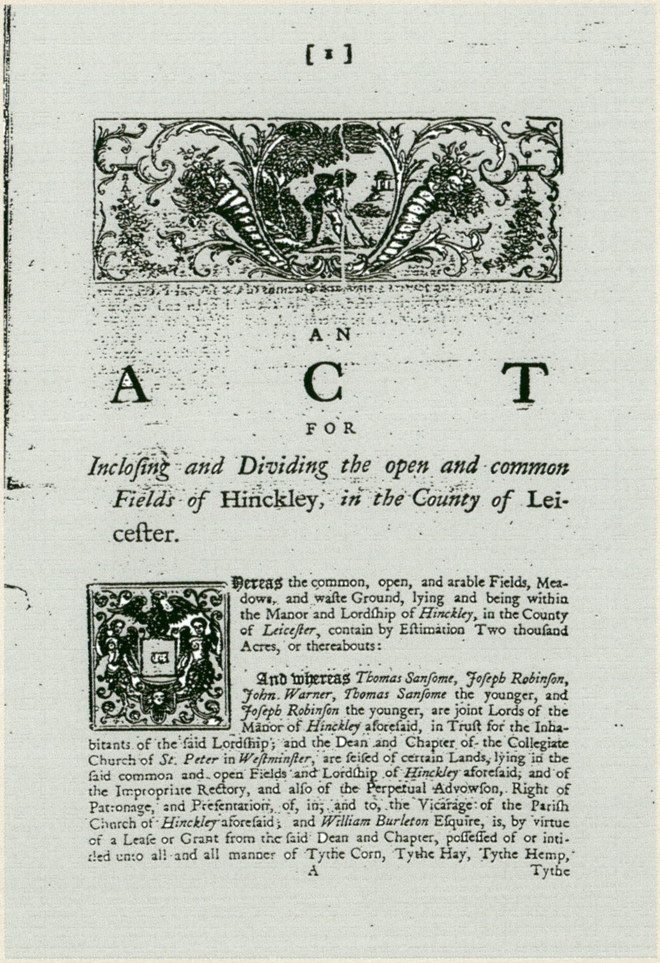
[1]

AN

ACT

FOR

Incloſing and Dividing the open and common Fields of Hinckley, *in the County of* Lei-ceſter.

Whereas the common, open, and arable Fields, Meadows, and waſte Ground, lying and being within the Manor and Lordſhip of *Hinckley*, in the County of *Leiceſter*, contain by Eſtimation Two thouſand Acres, or thereabouts:

And whereas *Thomas Sanſome, Joſeph Robinſon, John Warner, Thomas Sanſome* the younger, and *Joſeph Robinſon* the younger, are joint Lords of the Manor of *Hinckley* aforeſaid, in Truſt for the Inhabitants of the ſaid Lordſhip; and the Dean and Chapter of the Collegiate Church of *St. Peter* in *Weſtminſter*, are ſeiſed of certain Lands, lying in the ſaid common and open Fields and Lordſhip of *Hinckley* aforeſaid; and of the Impropriate Rectory, and alſo of the Perpetual Advowſon, Right of Patronage, and Preſentation, of, in, and to, the Vicarage of the Pariſh Church of *Hinckley* aforeſaid; and *William Burleton* Eſquire, is, by virtue of a Leaſe or Grant from the ſaid Dean and Chapter, poſſeſſed of or intitled unto all and all manner of Tythe Corn, Tythe Hay, Tythe Hemp,

A Tythe

First page of Hinckley's Enclosure Act, Leicester Records Office

It was the enclosure of the open fields and commons that created the countryside we know today and which some people think of as timeless, with isolated farmsteads and a patchwork of hedged fields interspersed with spinneys of trees. Hinckley was enclosed by an Act of Parliament of 1759, which was put into effect in 1760. It was probably at the instigation of larger landowners who wanted to consolidate their holdings in order to improve efficiency and thereby maximise profits in the newly emerging market for foodstuff for people in the growing towns and industrialising areas who produced none of their own. This is referred to in the Enclosure Act itself: "The land belonging to the freeholders, land-owners and proprietors of lands in the open and common fields of Hinckley do lie intermixed and dispersed in small parcels in and over the common fields and most of them inconveniently situated in respect to the houses of Hinckley" (13). This caused the problem "that a sufficient quantity of manure and compost could not without great difficulty and expense be conveyed" which itself was "a great difficulty to industry and improvement". Enclosure was going on all over England at an accelerated rate in the eighteenth century, especially in its later half. The changes which happened in Hinckley and the destruction of the medieval fields system and the social system that went with it, which had been gradually eroding since the sixteenth century, was typical of most villages during that time.

From parish registers, wills, tax and tithe lists and the enclosure award itself, it is possible to trace a number of Hinckley families back to pre-enclosure times and a few even as far back as the middle ages. Just because a local family name is absent from some of these early records does not necessarily mean that they were not part of the community. They may not have had any relevance to what was being documented in the remaining early records, which mostly relate to taxation of the minority of better off members of the community. The parish records

12 Anyone interested in this kind of farming community can visit Laxton in Nottinghamshire which is a village that has never been enclosed. It is England's last remaining community working an open field system.

go back to the mid sixteenth century when it became obligatory for churches to record baptisms, marriages and funerals. Even the very earliest entries in these registers form a list of Hinckley people whose family names are familiar in the area today. Many of these families later went into framework knitting and became the foundation of the local industry.

Enclosure gave the hosiery industry its launch towards modern productive relations. As the re-division of the open fields and common lands created individual farmsteads, those with rights to most property moved out of town to their own farms. Others received land and property within the town itself, either scattered holdings and allotments in lieu of former shares in the open fields and common, or exchanged plots with neighbours to create larger more workable consolidated plots. The relocation of some households to the countryside left some town centre farm buildings vacant, creating space for knitters and their frames to move into. A number of named individuals as well as "divers others being seised and possessed of several cottages within the Lordship of Hinckley, in respect thereof they were severally entitled to parcels of land" in and around the town in compensation for the loss of former rights. In this way, for example, Robert Atkins became the owner of land in the Bond End area of the town. Other names mentioned in the Enclosure Act, some of them already familiar in the story of Hinckley hosiery, are Joseph Robinson and his son, also called Joseph, Thomas Sansome who was the lord of the manor, William Hurst, Joseph Illiff (without an E so probably the son of John and Christian), Christopher Stephenson, Thomas Brown, Robert Lea, Henry Brierley, Samuel Craven, Michael Applebee, John Stevenson, Elizabeth Cotterel, Joseph Preston, Robert Bains (as in Bains Lane), John Farmer, Thomas Cooper, and Ann Williams, a widow. Many of these family names are familiar from recent oral history research and indicate that there is some continuity of residence in the community and also working in the hosiery trade over many generations. Asking people about their families in past generations together with research in the remaining archives indicates a very wide kinship network in the town. For example, a retired hosiery worker remembers her mother telling her that she was related to the Iliffe family. It is significant that those mentioned by name had title to land and property rights. This seems to have given them a head start in the developing industrial economy of the town. A good proportion of the family names of property owners in 1760 are later recognised as hosiers and then factory owners.

The Hinckley Enclosure Act and Award that created legal ownership of property can be examined in Leicestershire Record Office.

The Act made the individual land-owners responsible for the costs of administration and for the measuring and surveying entailed. They also had to bear the cost of erecting the fences, hedges and ditches around the reapportioned lands that created what present day people think of as the traditional English countryside around the town. Two hundred years ago this was not a traditional landscape but a strange and for many of those excluded from it for the first time, a hostile one that carried the risk of trespass if ventured on to. Mortgages were permitted to pay for all this expense but the costs must have been prohibitive for some of the smaller land-holders.

The people who had no or little property now lost their former rights to use the common land and may not have had enough or even any land around their homes to supply them with produce, which they probably rented from a larger land holder. These people would not have been able to survive without working for someone who was better off than they were themselves. Some of them would have stayed working in agriculture by becoming farm-servants. Enclosure although not directly related to the hosiery trade, can be seen as relevant and very important to its development as it created a pool of landless people whose only means of living was to sell their skills and labour power to those in a position to buy it. Because there were already a substantial number of people working as framework knitters, it would have been quite logical for those newly expropriated to turn to the trade for full-time employment. Many of them would already have been working part-time or seasonally in the cottage industry to supplement their agricultural endeavours. Some of those losing out on their former common rights could have received compensation or sold a very small plot to someone with a larger one who wished to consolidate his land to a more profitable size. This may have enabled some to purchase a frame or two. Many would have been too poor to do so and would have had no choice other than to hire one by renting it from someone who could afford to buy one or several and not work them themselves or within their immediate family. The enclosure award granted codified property to those with most land in pre-enclosure society and gave them advantages when it came to generating income and wealth in the new social system that replaced it. The award lists a number of names and what property they were entitled to. The descendants of these families often became familiar names in the local hosiery industry, frequently as hosiers. They became part of the capitalist class of employers in the town, owning or controlling as they now did the land itself and the means for others to make a livelihood by purchasing and renting out knitting frames and deciding what was produced and at what price. Although the stockingers worked in their own homes and in theory could choose the hours they worked, they could not control how much to sell their goods for, they did not own the raw materials or finished product and, usually, had no other means of subsistence. They had to produce as much or as little as the hosier dictated. Even in the domestic system they were wage labourers and not independent craftsmen.

THE ORGANISATION OF THE INDUSTRY

In the latter years of the eighteenth century the hosiery business seems to have been doing quite well. Industrialisation in other parts of the country created a demand for cheap ready-made stockings by workers who had no time to make their own clothes. This was especially true of the Lancashire textile producing areas in which there was a lot of employment of women. As well as this emerging mass market for cheap hose, there was also a demand for a more expensive quality product. It was the fashion amongst well-to-do men to wear knee length breeches, which were complemented by good quality, sometimes decorated, hose. These quality stockings were fully-fashioned, meaning they were knitted to shape on the machine by the knitter who reduced the number of stitches on a row at appropriate points. The knitted item then had to be seamed, that is sewn together to create a stocking. Sometimes decorative patterns known as "clocks" or "clox" were added at the ankle shaping, popular when the fashion for women's skirts became a little shorter at the beginning of the nineteenth century. Hinckley specialised in this quality fully-fashioned trade. Cotton was introduced as a raw material for knitting in the later eighteenth century. This cotton hose manufacture was centred in Hinckley, Burbage, Earl Shilton and Barwell. Leicester and the other county knitting villages produced mainly woollen stockings and later a cheaper product known as "cut-ups". These cut-up stockings were not fully-fashioned but knitted straight on the frame without any shaping. When wide frames were introduced several stockings could be made at the same time. The stockings were cut to shape afterwards and then sewn up by a seamer. This created a much cheaper though inferior product that did not last as long as the fully-fashioned items. This was because if the seam came unstitched the knitting would unravel as it had no selfedge. This made it much harder to repair. The differences in market specialisation would have a major effect in later years.

Knitting Frame which according to research by Bill Partridge of Hinckley is the oldest in existence.

Less than twenty years after enclosure Hinckley contained 864 knitting frames that employed 2,150 people. Of these 1,000 were framework knitters, 250 were seamers, 50 woolcombers, 28 framesmiths and 822 were spinners, doublers and twisters of the yarns used in manufacture (14). The nature of the early industry was always family based production, a proto-industrial cottage industry. The family was a productive unit - the men operated the frame although sometimes widows and single women did so too. As operating the frame was physically demanding women were normally involved in seaming and together with children twisting, doubling and winding the yarns. Twisting and doubling refer to processes performed on the yarns after spinning but before the wool or cotton was ready to be knitted up. No spinning was done at home, the knitter received it in hanks already spun from the hosier (15). A single yarn was too thin for most uses and so had to be doubled, that is two separate lengths of yarn had to be combined together. Twisting would put a twist into the yarn to hold the two or more strands together. This could be done in the home on a manually operated twisting mill.

Perhaps "family" production is not a strictly accurate term. Framework knitters took on children as apprentices to be brought up in the trade. These apprentices lived with the master knitter as part of his household as did some adult journeymen, so perhaps household production describes the situation better than family. This family or household unit of production was not made up of independent producers or craftsmen. The framework knitters were mostly employed by hosiers. The hosier would supply the yarn to the stockinger, who would receive payment according to how much he had knitted at a rate per dozen determined by the hosier. The hosier would then sell the finished stockings or other items. Therefore the framework knitter was a piece worker even in the domestic system.

In towns like Hinckley there were hosiers who supplied yarn from their warehouses or shops to the knitters or stockingers. Most Hinckley stockingers were able to deal directly with the hosier themselves as it was not far to go to collect the yarn and deliver the finished hose. John Biggs and Sons of Leicester had frames in a number of villages including Hinckley (16). In the villages in the surrounding area such as Stoke Golding, Burbage and Earl Shilton, where the knitters did not have easy access to the hosiers, a new role in the industry emerged, that of middlemen or putters out. These middlemen would collect the yarn from a hosier and take it to the individual stockingers. He would collect their finished stockings and pay them the rate offered by the hosier for it less, of course, a fee for himself. Another kind of middleman was known as an undertaker, who agreed with a hosier to arrange the making up of a specified amount of yarn for an agreed price. Obviously the stockingers who worked to enable him to fulfil his undertaking with the hosier were paid less than the undertaker himself received. A bag hosier was another kind of middleman who bought yarn from a number of different hosier's warehouses. The bag man put out the yarn to the knitters whom he paid for their work on collection of the finished goods. Bag hosiers sold the finished goods

14 - Felkin, Pickering

15 - Marilyn Palmer, Framework Knitting, Shire Album 119, 1984

16 - Victoria County History, History of Leicestershire, Vol III, p5

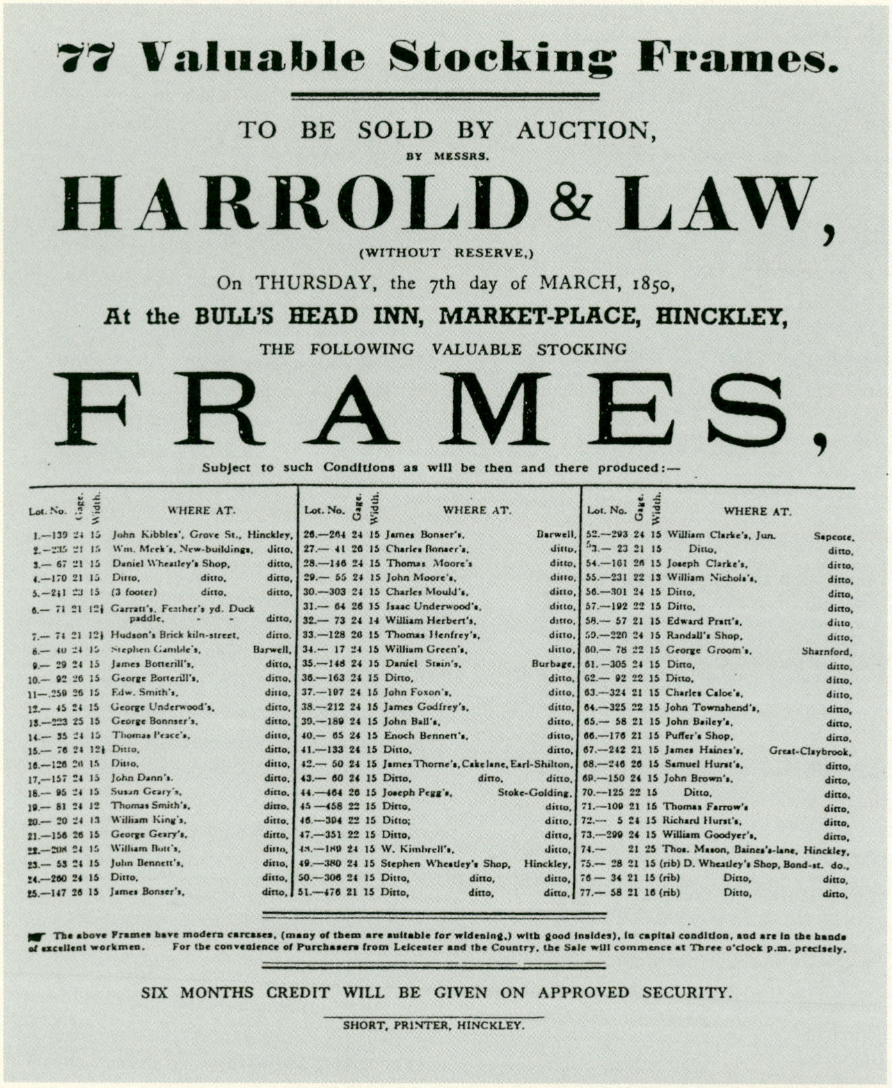

77 Valuable Stocking Frames.

TO BE SOLD BY AUCTION,

BY MESSRS.

HARROLD & LAW,

(WITHOUT RESERVE,)

On THURSDAY, the 7th day of MARCH, 1850,

At the BULL'S HEAD INN, MARKET-PLACE, HINCKLEY,

THE FOLLOWING VALUABLE STOCKING

FRAMES,

Subject to such Conditions as will be then and there produced:—

Lot. No.	Gage.	Width.	WHERE AT.	
1.—139	24	15	John Kibbles', Grove St.,	Hinckley,
2.—235	21	15	Wm. Meek's, New-buildings,	ditto,
3.— 67	21	15	Daniel Wheatley's Shop,	ditto,
4.—170	21	15	Ditto, ditto,	ditto,
5.—241	23	15	(3 footer) ditto,	ditto,
6.— 71	21	12½	Garratt's, Feather's yd. Duck paddle, - -	ditto,
7.— 74	21	12½	Hudson's Brick kiln-street,	ditto.
8.— 40	24	15	Stephen Gamble's,	Barwell,
9.— 29	24	15	James Botterill's,	ditto,
10.— 92	26	15	George Botterill's,	ditto,
11—.259	26	15	Edw. Smith's,	ditto,
12.— 45	24	15	George Underwood's,	ditto,
13.—223	25	15	George Bonnser's,	ditto,
14.— 35	24	15	Thomas Peace's,	ditto,
15.— 76	24	12½	Ditto,	ditto,
16.—126	26	15	Ditto,	ditto,
17.—157	24	15	John Dann's.	ditto,
18.— 95	24	15	Susan Geary's,	ditto,
19.— 81	24	12	Thomas Smith's,	ditto,
20.— 20	24	13	William King's,	ditto,
21.—156	26	15	George Geary's,	ditto,
22.—208	24	15	William Bott's,	ditto,
23.— 53	24	15	John Bennett's,	ditto,
24.—260	24	15	Ditto,	ditto,
25.—147	26	15	James Bonser's,	ditto,

Lot. No.	Gage.	Width.	WHERE AT.	
26.—264	24	15	James Bonser's,	Barwell,
27.— 41	26	15	Charles Bonser's,	ditto,
28.—146	24	15	Thomas Moore's	ditto,
29.— 55	24	15	John Moore's,	ditto,
30.—303	24	15	Charles Mould's,	ditto,
31.— 64	26	15	Isaac Underwood's,	ditto,
32.— 73	24	14	William Herbert's,	ditto,
33.—128	26	15	Thomas Henfrey's,	ditto,
34.— 17	24	15	William Green's,	ditto,
35.—148	24	15	Daniel Stain's,	Burbage,
36.—163	24	15	Ditto,	ditto,
37.—107	24	15	John Foxon's,	ditto,
38.—212	24	15	James Godfrey's,	ditto,
39.—189	24	15	John Ball's,	ditto,
40.— 65	24	15	Enoch Bennett's,	ditto,
41.—133	24	15	Ditto,	ditto,
42.— 50	24	15	James Thorne's, Cake lane,	Earl-Shilton,
43.— 60	24	15	Ditto, ditto,	ditto,
44.—464	26	15	Joseph Pegg's,	Stoke-Golding,
45—458	22	15	Ditto,	ditto,
46.—394	22	15	Ditto;	ditto,
47.—351	22	15	Ditto,	ditto,
48.—189	24	15	W. Kimbrell's,	ditto,
49.—380	24	15	Stephen Wheatley's Shop,	Hinckley,
50.—306	24	15	Ditto, ditto,	ditto,
51.—476	21	15	Ditto, ditto,	ditto,

Lot. No.	Gage.	Width.	WHERE AT.	
52.—293	24	15	William Clarke's, Jun.	Sapcote,
53.— 23	21	15	Ditto,	ditto,
54.—161	26	15	Joseph Clarke's,	ditto,
55.—231	22	13	William Nichols's,	ditto,
56.—301	24	15	Ditto,	ditto,
57.—192	22	15	Ditto,	ditto,
58.— 57	21	15	Edward Pratt's,	ditto,
59.—220	24	15	Randall's Shop,	ditto,
60.— 78	22	15	George Groom's,	Sharnford,
61.—305	24	15	Ditto,	ditto,
62.— 92	22	15	Ditto,	ditto,
63.—324	21	15	Charles Caloe's,	ditto,
64.—325	22	15	John Townshend's,	ditto,
65.— 58	21	15	John Bailey's,	ditto,
66.—176	21	15	Puffer's Shop,	ditto,
67.—242	21	15	James Haines's,	Great-Claybrook,
68.—246	26	15	Samuel Hurst's,	ditto,
69.—150	24	15	John Brown's,	ditto,
70.—125	22	15	Ditto,	ditto,
71.—109	21	15	Thomas Farrow's	ditto,
72.— 5	24	15	Richard Hurst's,	ditto,
73.—299	24	15	William Goodyer's,	ditto,
74.—	21	25	Thos. Mason, Baines's-lane,	Hinckley,
75.— 28	21	15 (rib)	D. Wheatley's Shop, Bond-st.	do.,
76 — 34	21	15 (rib)	Ditto,	ditto,
77.— 58	21	16 (rib)	Ditto,	ditto,

The above Frames have modern carcases, (many of them are suitable for widening,) with good insides), in capital condition, and are in the hands of excellent workmen. For the convenience of Purchasers from Leicester and the Country, the Sale will commence at Three o'clock p.m. precisely.

SIX MONTHS CREDIT WILL BE GIVEN ON APPROVED SECURITY.

SHORT, PRINTER, HINCKLEY.

List of Stocking Frames for sale by auction showing they are placed with various people.

themselves to retail warehouses and did not undertake work for any specific hosier. The distributors buying from bagmen were known as "turkey merchants" amongst the knitters (17). Ironically some bagmen obtained yarn from framework knitters who had embezzled it from other hosiers (18) in order to make a bit of extra money on the side. These middlemen took on the role of employer as the knitters had no direct relationship with the hosier. In the villages where knitters were forced to accept the services of a middleman the rates paid were much lower than in the town of Hinckley which in turn were lower than in Leicester. This caused problems for all the knitters in the trade as they either received less than the going rate for the work if they were in villages or were constantly undercut by those in the villages working for lower rates if they lived in town. Out of 217 frames worked in Stoke Golding ten worked for Leicester hosiers and the remainder for bagmen and middlemen from Hinckley (19). Hinckley knitters were undercut by knitters in the surrounding villages and they themselves undercut the better paid workers in Leicester.

Despite their dubious methods of conducting business, bag-hosiers did at least provide work for the knitters. According to William Wykes, a middleman of Hinckley, if the bagmen had not set up there "there would not have been any employment in the town. Those people used to go to Leicester and fetch work and they the hosiers of Leicester got them (ie the bagmen) to work for them at certain times" (20).

Most of those in the hosiery industry could not afford to buy their own frame. For this reason they were forced to rent one from a hosier or middleman. This meant whatever they were paid for their work they had to make a fixed payment for frame rent which was deducted from their earnings. The amount knitters paid in rent could have paid for the frame many times over. People not connected with the trade, such as shopkeepers and inn keepers, saw this as an opportunity for a profitable investment and purchased frames which they hired to hosiers and middlemen who sublet them at a profit to the knitters. This guaranteed the owner, the hosier or the middleman an income even in the worst of slumps when trade was appalling. In the same situation it was a guarantee of poverty for the knitter who had to pay the frame rent whether or not he was earning anything at all. Richard Wileman of Earl Shilton, who had passed through the ranks from framework knitter himself, owned between 200 and 300 frames in 1845 that were let out to the hands he employed (21). Frame rents tied the knitter to work for only one hosier or middleman as only work put out by them was allowed to be worked on the frame. This prevented rates of pay being augmented by competition for labour from better paying employers. It also meant that when there was little demand for their products, instead of freeing some of the knitters from frame rents, the amount of yarn put out was shared between all the knitters to ensure income from the rental was still forthcoming to the masters. When the employers "stinted" them the knitters were all working for less and less. Not only did hosiers and middlemen profit from the labour of the knitters who worked for them, they also gained profits on the actual means

17 - Pickering, p67
18 - Victoria County History, p9
19 - Victoria County History, p5
20 - First Appendix to the Report on the Condition of Framework Knitters, 1845, p204; Victoria County History, p9
21 - First Appendix to the Report on the Condition of Framework Knitters, 1845, p244; Victoria County History, p11

of production itself which in other industries would have become a depreciating asset. Some framework knitters who owned their own frames sold them in order to rent them back to guarantee a supply of work from a hosier or middleman.

The knitters also bore the unavoidable expenses of needles and oil for the frame and fuel to provide lighting in the form of candles and coal for heating the work room. Perhaps these injustices were the reason framework knitters had a reputation for dishonesty amongst the employers. One way the knitters used to get their own back on the employers was by "scotch misting" which meant dampening the yarn, perhaps using steam, to increase its weight and, the extra yarn embezzled like this could be sold on to a bagman. As they worked unsupervised the knitters could determine their own hours of work. Many chose to take time off at the beginning of the week when they were paid, making up for lost time by working long hours towards the end of the week and perhaps through Friday night to get the work ready for collection. An Act of Parliament of 1777 tried to prevent outdoor workers from defrauding their employers, who had no way of supervising the worker in his or her home to make sure that he actually applied himself to his work. This legislation stated that "if work was put out in the textile trades, for example in the hatting, woollen, linen, fustian, cotton, leather, fur, hemp, flax, mohair and silk industries, should anyone hired, retained or employed to prepare or work up any materials whether mixed or unmixed for any master shall wilfully neglect or refuse the performance thereof for 8 days consecutively such person being thereof lawfully convicted shall be imprisoned not exceeding six months nor less than one". Leicester hosiers tried to prosecute village outworkers, to whom they had put out work, for fraud in the 1830's using this Act. However, they lost their case because the Act referred only to workers in the same borough not in villages, like those around Hinckley to where they put out work at undercutting rates (22).

Another method used by the employers to exploit their labour force was the truck system. Often the frames were owned by shopkeepers or the hosier also owned or had family with a shop. Bag-hosiers were often also shop-keepers, the profit from selling food could be used to buy frames to let out. Truck meant that instead of being paid cash, the knitter was paid in kind, either with goods or tokens which could only be exchanged in the truck-master's shop. The prices were inflated but the shopkeepers could get away with their extortion as the knitter was not in a position to shop around and take his or his family's custom elsewhere. Although made illegal in 1831 this method of both oppression and exploitation was difficult to eradicate for many years. In Earl Shilton most of the small grocers held frames and acted as middlemen. In evidence to the Commission of Inquiry into the Condition of the Framework Knitters, Isaac Abbott, a knitter from the village stated "they give out their work the same as the other hosiers and they take it in the same". "They do not perhaps take it in the grocery shop, but they have a room above-stairs where they take in the work, and pay the hands their money in that room, and the hands have to pass through the shop in coming out of that room, and there they lay out their money or pay off the bill for the goods they had the previous week" (23). If challenged on the legality of this practice the hosier cum shop keeper could always claim that the hands chose to use the shop and could make their purchases elsewhere if they chose. However, if they did they might not be in such a secure position regarding future work. Through the exploitation of the knitters using means other than just profit margins on the work they did, the employers were able to take much of the risk out of business as they were guaranteed an income from frame rents even if there was little profit to be had selling the finished products. They had guaranteed customers for their shop in which they did not even need to be concerned about competitive pricing or the quality of the goods. As well as unfair to the stockingers, the truck system was also looked upon as unfair to manufacturers who paid their workers in coin. No wonder that the hosiery industry was one of the last to move into factories, the employers were on to too good a thing to want to change things. Meanwhile, poverty amongst framework knitters, (who even before that had always been subject to the trade cycle, sometimes adversely, sometimes advantageously), became endemic by the 1820's.

22 Document in Leicestershire Records Office, Acc no DG5/850

23 1st App to Rep on Condition of Framework Knitters, p284

APPRENTICESHIPS, POVERTY AND MIGRATORY LABOUR - THE GROWTH OF HINCKLEY

The latter years of the eighteenth century were relatively affluent for the hosiery industry, compared with what was to come during most of the nineteenth century. It seemed a healthy trade to join and families who were able to afford the indenture fee were willing to pay for their sons to learn "the mysteries of the trade".

To become an apprentice, a young person's parent or guardian had to pay a fee to a master framework knitter who was himself "time-served", meaning he also had served an apprenticeship. The fees paid were sometimes quite high, ranging from £3. 3s (3 guineas) to £6. 6s (6 guineas), quite a substantial sum in those days. A legal agreement, the indenture, was signed between the parent or guardian of the child who could have been as young as 8 or as old as 14, 15 or 16. The indenture stated that the apprentice would serve his or her master until reaching the age of 21 or even 24 when they "came out of their time". During this period they would learn the skills of the trade and work at different tasks given them. The little children probably began by winding, doubling and twisting the yarn ready for use on the frames and seaming the finished stockings before they were big enough to start work on the frame which was quite large and heavy. Other jobs would have been keeping the fire lit to ensure a constant temperature, general household tasks and running errands (an outdoor activity that could also have presented opportunities for play). The apprentices would live as part of the master's household and be fed and clothed as they might have been by a parent. The terms of the indenture often forbade the apprentice from leaving the master's house without permission, visiting taverns and alehouses, playing cards and dice, going to theatres, fornication and contracting to marry. This would not have been any hardship for an eight year old but might have been problematic for the older apprentices as they reached young adulthood, in those days at the age of 21. In theory the system of apprenticeship should have given framework knitters some protection against too many people in the trade, too much competition in the labour market and hence lower rates of pay for the job.

Sending children as young as eight away from their family and home, often to a different town or village and setting it to work in a trade where conditions were fairly harsh, with no right to leave if they didn't like it, may seem cruel by modern standards. Children nowadays, though, are forced to go to school to learn subjects in which they have no immediate interest, when they might rather be doing something else. Both the apprenticeship system and, since the early 1870s, the compulsory education system have tried to serve the needs of society by creating people with appropriate skills and attitudes for the productive system of the time.

As the capacity of the hosiery trade increased the only way to increase output and profits using manually operated machines was to increase the number of workers. The capacity of the trade grew and along with it the number of apprentices taken on. The initial success of the trade led not just to families seeing it as a potentially lucrative occupation for their children. The parish poor law authorities saw it as a means to get pauper children off their hands. For them the apprenticeship of the children of the

Single bobbin winder - Wigston Framework Knitters Museum. This machine could be operated by a child turning the handle.

poor or orphans from the workhouse represented a way of reducing their costs for both outdoor relief (help given to poor people who remained living in their own homes) and indoor relief (where the poor person lived in an institution called the workhouse). This would bring down the costs of the poor rates paid by better-off parish residents. Pauper children provided a pool of cheap labour for the growing textile trades, not just in hosiery but in ribbon weaving and the woollen and cotton industries. The tough conditions and poor health of the pauper apprentices and the suffering caused by child labour in factories was later exposed especially in the cotton mills by Factory Commission Reports. Restricting the hours of work and providing some form of education for factory children became a cause celèbre of Tory reformers like Lord Shaftesbury, sometimes as a political attack on the mostly Whig factory owners. The Factory Acts did not apply to the hosiery industry, which was domestic and then later workshop and not factory based, until after the 1850s. Children working in hosiery and knitting were therefore exempt from the Factory Acts and their conditions of work not so well documented.

The guardians of the poor in Leicestershire and Warwickshire parishes acted as procurers of child labour not just for the Leicestershire hosiery industry but also the ribbon weaving industry of Warwickshire. Poor Law records reveal that children from Leicestershire, especially the north and south western part of the county, were apprenticed to ribbon weavers in northern Warwickshire. At the same time the guardians in north Warwickshire were sending some of their pauper children to the Hinckley area to work in the framework knitting industry. The Congreve family of Ratcliffe Culey, on the edge of Leicestershire's border with Warwickshire, had a boy called Thomas who was 12 in 1800 apprenticed to Edward Gunton, a framesmith of Hinckley and a girl, Mary, aged 13 in 1811 apprenticed to a ribbon-weaver of Witherley, Thomas White.

By examining the records of the Leicestershire parish poor law authorities it is easy to see that between 1760 and 1815, although there are earlier and later examples, the majority of pauper children apprenticed were indentured to framework knitters, a substantial proportion of whom were sent to the Hinckley area, including Earl Shilton. These records can also be used to compile a list of framework knitters already in the trade during that period and also some of those moving to Hinckley because of the hosiery industry and thereby contributing to the economic development of the town and its major trade.

Taking on apprentices seems to have been a lucrative business itself as a master knitter could expect quite large sums as premiums, up to £6. 6s in some cases for each child taken on. Some of these masters' names are repeated many times in the records, indicating that they had quite a large group of indentured children living and working with them for whom they had received payment as well as the opportunity to exploit their labour. Leire and Lutterworth were major exporters of children. In some cases whole families were sent to the same master. The children of James Bishop of Sharnford, for example, Thomas, John and William were all apprenticed to John King of Earl Shilton. Thomas went in 1803 at the age of thirteen, followed by 10 year old William in 1805. They were then joined by John their younger brother in 1807 when he too reached the age of ten.

The children of Thomas Button, a labourer of Desford were not so lucky. They were split up. In 1805 Ann Button was apprenticed to Daniel Allsop, a Hinckley framework knitter to learn housewifery. Mary Button who was 10 in 1807 was apprenticed to another knitter, Samuel Best in Earl Shilton. She would not have been too lonely as after two years Best took in another

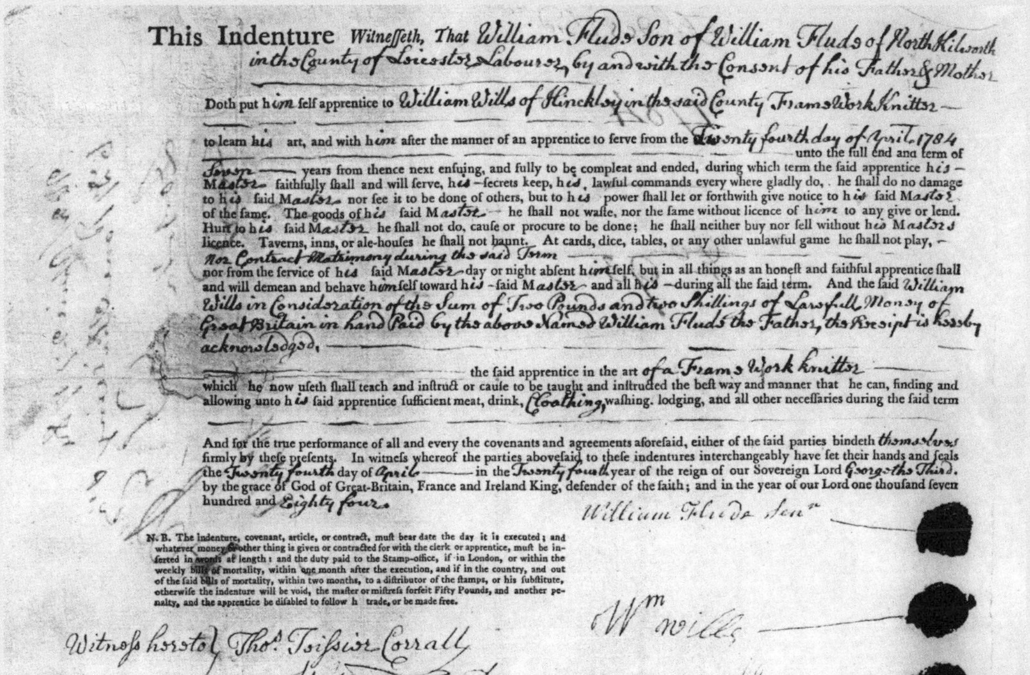

This Indenture Witneſſeth, That William Flude Son of William Flude of North Kilworth in the County of Leicester Labourer, by and with the Consent of his Father & Mother

Doth put him ſelf apprentice to William Wills of Hinckley in the said County Frame Work Knitter

to learn his art, and with him after the manner of an apprentice to ſerve from the Twenty fourth day of April 1784 unto the full end and term of Seven years from thence next enſuing, and fully to be compleat and ended, during which term the ſaid apprentice his Master faithfully ſhall and will ſerve, his ſecrets keep, his lawful commands every where gladly do, . he ſhall do no damage to his ſaid Master nor ſee it to be done of others, but to his power ſhall let or forthwith give notice to his ſaid Master of the ſame. The goods of his ſaid Master he ſhall not waſte, nor the ſame without licence of him to any give or lend. Hurt to his ſaid Master he ſhall not do, cauſe or procure to be done; he ſhall neither buy nor ſell without his Masters licence. Taverns, inns, or ale-houſes he ſhall not haunt. At cards, dice, tables, or any other unlawful game he ſhall not play, nor Contract Matrimony during the said Term nor from the ſervice of his ſaid Master day or night abſent himſelf, but in all things as an honeſt and faithful apprentice ſhall and will demean and behave himſelf toward his ſaid Master and all his during all the ſaid term. And the ſaid William Wills in Consideration of the Sum of Two Pounds and two Shillings of Lawfull Money of Great Britain in hand Paid by the above Named William Flude the Father, the Receipt is hereby acknowledged,

the ſaid apprentice in the art of a Frame Work knitter which he now uſeth ſhall teach and inſtruct or cauſe to be taught and inſtructed the beſt way and manner that he can, finding and allowing unto his ſaid apprentice ſufficient meat, drink, Cloathing, waſhing. lodging, and all other neceſſaries during the ſaid term

And for the true performance of all and every the covenants and agreements aforeſaid, either of the ſaid parties bindeth themselves firmly by theſe preſents. In witneſs whereof the parties aboveſaid to theſe indentures interchangeably have ſet their hands and ſeals the Twenty fourth day of April in the Twenty fourth year of the reign of our Sovereign Lord George the Third. by the grace of God of Great-Britain, France and Ireland King, defender of the faith; and in the year of our Lord one thouſand ſeven hundred and Eighty four.

William Flude Senr

N. B. The indenture, covenant, article, or contract, muſt bear date the day it is executed; and whatever money or other thing is given or contracted for with the clerk or apprentice, muſt be inſerted in words at length: and the duty paid to the Stamp-office, if in London, or within the weekly bills of mortality, within one month after the execution, and if in the country, and out of the ſaid bills of mortality, within two months, to a diſtributor of the ſtamps, or his ſubſtitute, otherwiſe the indenture will be void, the maſter or miſtreſs forfeit Fifty Pounds, and another penalty, and the apprentice be diſabled to follow h trade, or be made free.

Witness hereto Thos. Trisier Corrall

William Mott

Wm Wills

Will m Flude

Indenture of William Flude of North Kilworth to William Wills of Hinckley - Leicester Records Office

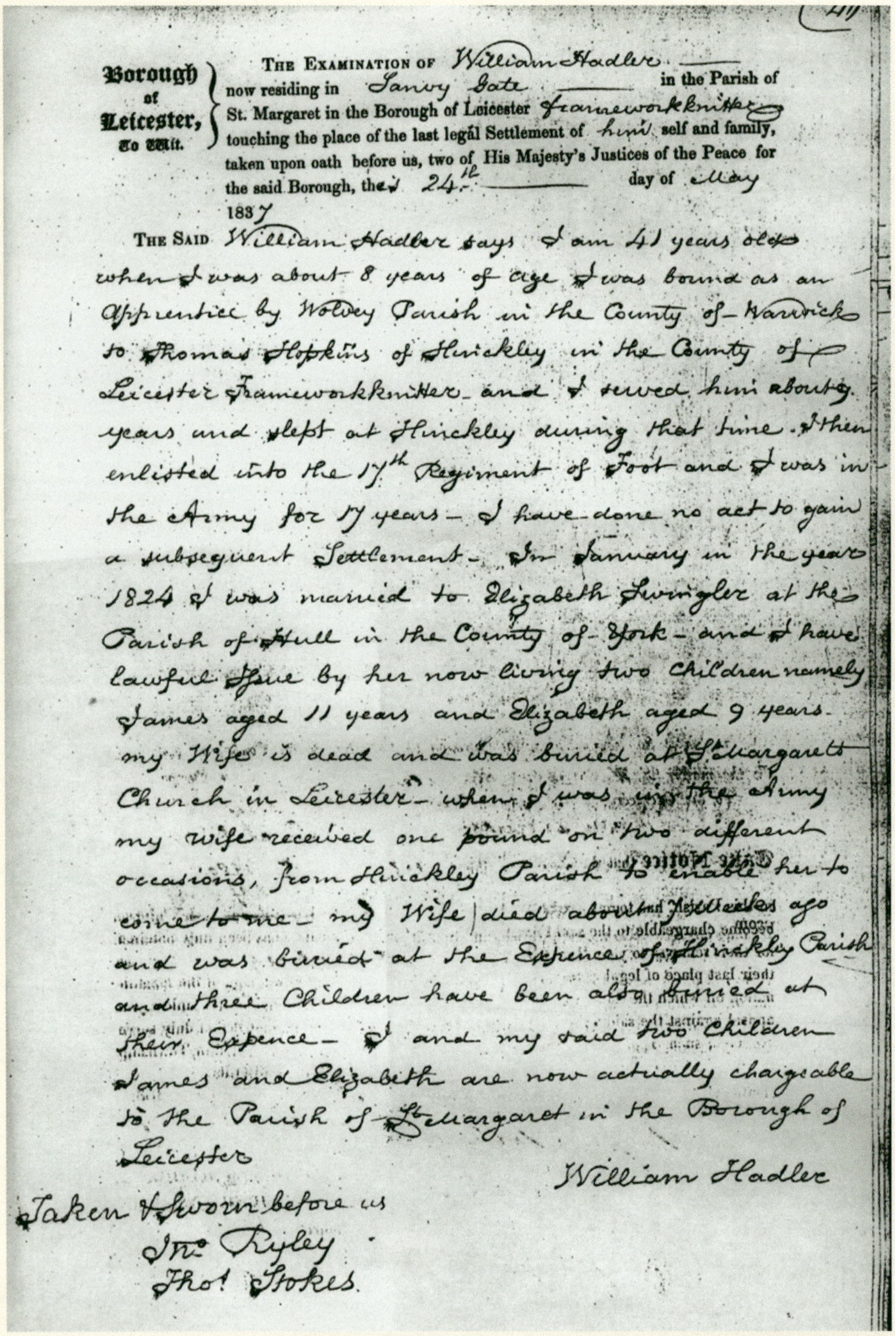

Borough of Leicester, To Wit.

The Examination of William Hadler now residing in Sanvy Gate in the Parish of St. Margaret in the Borough of Leicester Frameworkknitter touching the place of the last legal Settlement of him self and family, taken upon oath before us, two of His Majesty's Justices of the Peace for the said Borough, the 24th day of May 1837

The Said William Hadler says I am 41 years old when I was about 8 years of age I was bound as an Apprentice by Wolvey Parish in the County of Warwick to Thomas Hopkins of Hinckley in the County of Leicester Frameworkknitter and I served him about 9 years and slept at Hinckley during that time. I then enlisted into the 17th Regiment of Foot and I was in the Army for 17 years – I have done no act to gain a subsequent Settlement – In January in the year 1824 I was married to Elizabeth Swingler at the Parish of Hull in the County of York – and I have lawful Issue by her now living two Children namely James aged 11 years and Elizabeth aged 9 years. my Wife is dead and was buried at St Margarets Church in Leicester – when I was in the Army my wife received one pound on two different occasions, from Hinckley Parish to enable her to come to me – my Wife died about [illegible] weeks ago and was buried at the Expence of Hinckley Parish and three Children have been also buried at their Expence – I and my said two Children James and Elizabeth are now actually chargeable to the Parish of St Margaret in the Borough of Leicester

William Hadler

Taken & Sworn before us
Jno Ryley
Thos Stokes

Settlement Examination of William Hodler, 1837, LRO

little girl, 9 year old Mary Elliott. Perhaps Mary was big enough to work on the frame by then and he needed another child for the lighter jobs. The following year, 1808, 10 year old Benjamin and 8 year old John went together to Deverex Abbotts again in Earl Shilton to be trained as framework knitters. The family's situation does not seem to have improved over the next six years as in 1814 Thomas Button junior was apprenticed to another knitter, John Knight of Thurlaston. Thomas Bassett in 1807 had an apprentice who was almost grown up, Thomas Barrett, who had joined him in 1800. Two brothers joined the workshop, John and William Elliott, the sons of a poor custom-weaver, James, from Attleborough. Where children were not all placed with the same master they were often fortunate enough to be in the same town or village community which must have helped maintain family links. Using only this quantitative data it is not possible to tell whether this was an act of kindness to keep brothers and sisters together on the part of the guardians and masters or merely a financial transaction aimed at getting as many paupers off the parish's expense sheet as possible and, for the knitters, maximising the potential for exploitation. As well as an employer and a teacher, the framework knitter and his wife also acted as foster parents to these children. It is not possible to tell how the apprenticed children were treated in the household, in comparison with the knitters' own children, who might also have been set to work in the trade at an early age. Whatever their motives these knitters and their apprentices formed the nucleus of the new industrial town of Hinckley.

Sadly, the aspirations of the guardians of the poor and of the hosiers, knitters and the apprentices themselves were dashed within a generation, partly as a result of their own myopic optimism. The huge influx of framework knitters meant that when the economic situation changed from around 1815 onwards due to a number of factors there were just too many people in the

Hinckley trade for the demand for its products. The reasons for this decline in demand include the new fashion of wearing trousers instead of breeches by men who no longer required high quality, decorated stockings as they were no longer worn to be visible. Another factor was the decline in demand from the military after the Napoleonic wars reached their conclusion. A further exacerbation caused by peace in Europe was the returning home of former soldiers, of which Hinckley had contributed more than its share, seeking employment. There were stories of framework knitters during the wars having received a premium for taking on an apprentice, then "selling" him to a recruiting sergeant for an enlistment fee and then taking on yet another apprentice (24). Quite a profitable trade in human life!

Even when trade was bad and times were hard, hosiers and middlemen still required their frame-rents and so they spread less work between the same number of knitters who were able to earn less and less as they attempted to compete for work. This practice was known as stinting. Occasionally discontent would erupt into riots and demonstrations against the employers and other symbols of authority.

This poverty meant that a large number of dependent child apprentices was now a burden on the knitters, not a source of profit. Even for the better-off people and the hosiers themselves, times were getting harder as there was not only a decline in profits but a massive increase in the poor rates which had to be paid to support all the unemployed and underemployed people now in poverty. All those who had had apprenticeships, by the fact of having "served their time" were now able to claim settlement in Hinckley or its neighbouring knitting parishes and therefore claim relief from the parish in times of need.

All those settlements gained through serving an apprenticeship to a Hinckley area framework knitter became a burden to the community and a massive drain on the parish funds by the time that generation had grown up and had families of their own. Once hey had completed their

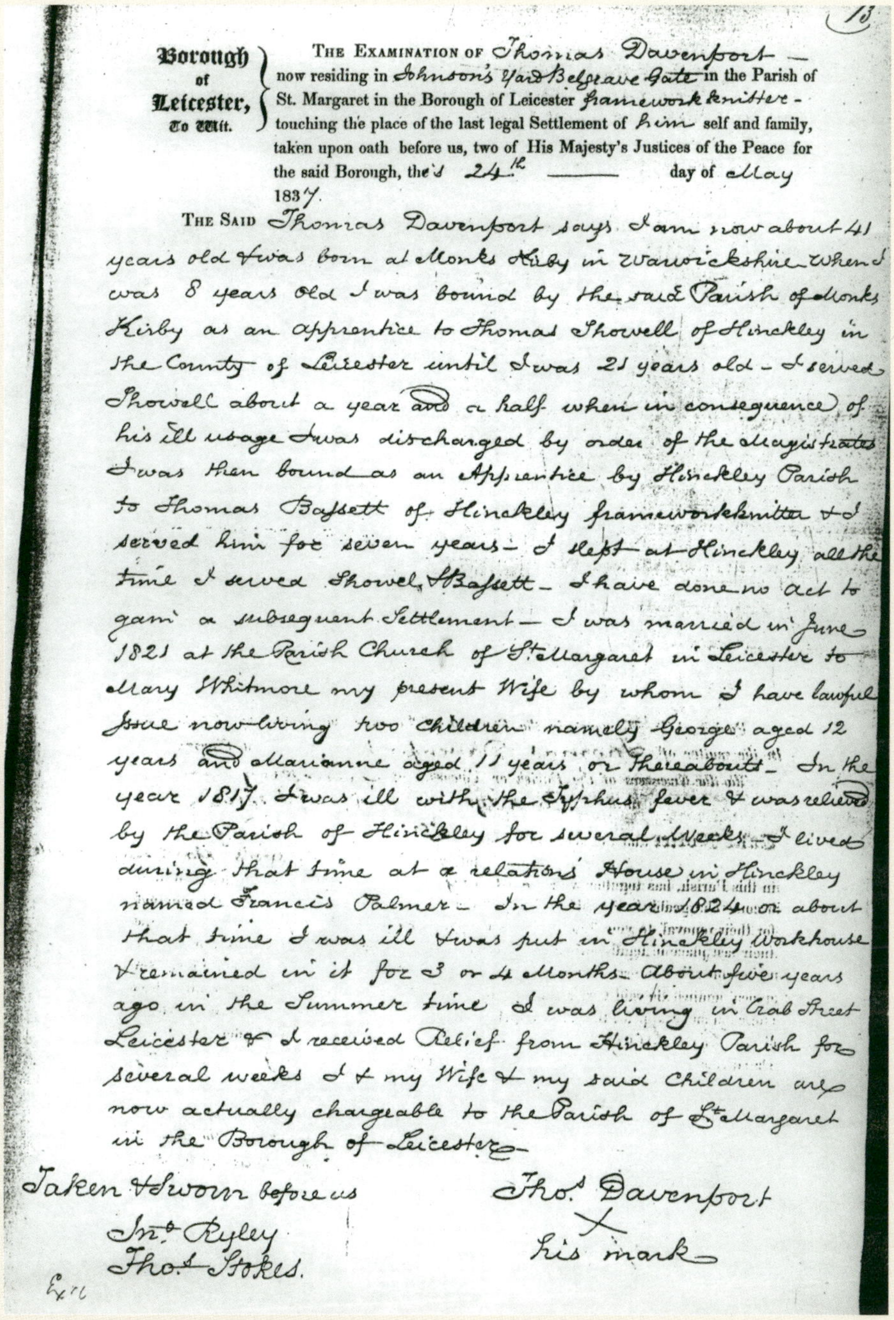

13

Borough of Leicester, To Wit. THE EXAMINATION OF Thomas Davenport — now residing in Johnson's Yard Belgrave Gate in the Parish of St. Margaret in the Borough of Leicester framework knitter - touching the place of the last legal Settlement of him self and family, taken upon oath before us, two of His Majesty's Justices of the Peace for the said Borough, the 24th day of May 1837.

THE SAID Thomas Davenport says I am now about 41 years old & was born at Monks Kirby in Warwickshire When I was 8 years old I was bound by the said Parish of Monks Kirby as an apprentice to Thomas Showell of Hinckley in the County of Leicester until I was 21 years old - I served Showell about a year and a half when in consequence of his ill usage I was discharged by order of the Magistrates I was then bound as an Apprentice by Hinckley Parish to Thomas Bassett of Hinckley frameworkknitter & I served him for seven years - I slept at Hinckley all the time I served Showell & Bassett - I have done no act to gain a subsequent Settlement - I was married in June 1821 at the Parish Church of St Margaret in Leicester to Mary Whitmore my present Wife by whom I have lawful Issue now living two children namely George aged 12 years and Marianne aged 11 years or thereabouts - In the year 1817 I was ill with the Typhus fever & was relieved by the Parish of Hinckley for several Weeks - I lived during that time at a relations' House in Hinckley named Francis Palmer - In the year 1824 or about that time I was ill & was put in Hinckley Workhouse & remained in it for 3 or 4 Months - About five years ago in the Summer time I was living in Crab Street Leicester & I received Relief from Hinckley Parish for several weeks I & my Wife & my said Children are now actually chargeable to the Parish of St Margaret in the Borough of Leicester -

Taken & Sworn before us
Jno Ryley
Thos Stokes

Thos Davenport
X
his mark

Exd

Settlement examination of Thomas Davenport, 1837, LRO

24 *Pickering, p122*

25 *Wages and Food of Leicestershire Framework Knitters 1815-1841, table given in William Biggs Scrapbook, LRO*

WAGES AND FOOD OF LEICESTER FRAMEWORK KNITTERS, 1815 TO 1841

	Price per dozen 24 gage hose 24 leads wide	Price of corn per quarter per quarter each year
1815	7s 6d	63s 8d
1816	7s 0d	76s 2d
1817	6s 0d	94s 0d
1818	6s 0d	83s 8d
1819	7s 0d	72s 3d
1820	7s 0d	65s 10d
1821	6s 6d	54s 5d
1822	6s 6d	43s 3d
1823	6s 6d	51s 9d
1824	5s 6d	62s 0d
1825	6s 6d	66s 6s
1826	5s 6d	56s 11d
1827	5s 6d	56s 9d
1828	5s 0d	60s 5d
1829	5s 0d	66s 3d
1830	5s 0d	64s 3d
1831	5s 0d	66s 4d
1832	4s 9d	58s 8d
1833	5s 0d	52s 11d
1834	4s 9d	46s 2d
1835	4s 9d	39s 4d
1836	5s 0d	48s 6d
1837	4s 9d	55s 10d
1838	4s 6d	64s 4d
1839	4s 6d	70s 6d
1840	4s 6d	66s 4d
1841	4s 6d	64s 6d

Figures given in the William Biggs Scrapbook, LRO

apprenticeships some of them had gone away to join the forces or worked as journeymen locally or in other knitting communities. Many moved to Leicester where trade initially was not so badly affected as the fully-fashioned work of Hinckley. But soon Leicester's knitting industry slumped as well. After the New Poor Law Act of 1834, all those claiming parish relief were only eligible if they went back to their "home" parish of settlement and, if they were able-bodied, should only be eligible if they were destitute and desperate enough to go in the workhouse. Outdoor relief became much harder to obtain. In the 1830's the price paid to stockingers for finished hose fell to an all time low and from the mid 1830's the price of corn, a staple foodstuff, rose sharply. The years 1837, 1838, 1839 and 1840 were particularly bad years, heralding what became known as "the hungry forties". From the table of prices for 24 gage (sic) hose and corn it can be seen that in 1837 the price per dozen for stockings was 4s 9d while corn cost 55s 10d a quarter. The knitters' pay had fallen from 5s a dozen the previous year, while the price of corn had gone up from 48s 6d per quarter. Things got worse over the next few years; in 1838 the amount received for hose went down to 4s 6d a dozen and stayed at that rate until at least 1841 when the table referred to was compiled (25). Food prices rocketed in 1838 to 64s 4d per quarter for corn and again the following year when it cost 70s 6d. In 1840 and 1841 corn cost 66shillings and 4d and 64shillings and 6d respectively, hardly any improvement for the poor stockingers. The drastic decline in stockingers' living standards after the Napoleonic wars is easily judged when these figures are compared with the year 1815 when the rate per dozen for hose was 7s 6d with the price of corn at 63s 8d per quarter.

The poor law records of St Margarets and All Saints parishes in Leicester show that in 1836, 1837 and 1838 the majority of those giving evidence in settlement examinations to determine which parish should provide relief, were framework knitters settled in the Hinckley area. Many of them had not been born there but they or even their fathers had served apprenticeships in the town making them legally settled there. Even widows whose only connection with the place might have been their father-in-law's apprenticeship were subject to "removal orders" making them the responsibility of Hinckley parish to where they must return if they wanted any assistance. As well as a tragedy for the poor people being forced to leave their homes through an order of removal, it was a huge burden on the poor-rate payers of Hinckley for whom the amount of rates payable went up phenomenally, just when trade was at its worst.

The poor law records reveal whole life-cycles of poverty for the framework knitters. Many of them were the children of paupers born at a time of rural distress due to the loss of rights caused by enclosure. Where the father's occupation is noted, labourer, meaning agricultural worker, is the most frequently stated. They were sent by the guardians of the poor in their home villages to work in Hinckley as apprenticed knitters until reaching the age of twenty-one. Some of their testimonies to the boards of guardians reveal that they were sometimes forced to leave their masters because of his poverty and shortages of work. Others ran away or joined the army while still children. John Sheen, aged 35, giving evidence in a settlement examination in 1837 told the guardians of St Margaret's parish in Leicester that he had been apprenticed to Sherrard Ford of Hinckley but his master had run away. John Dann in a statement to the same board of guardians said that he was 62 years old and had been born in Walsingham in Norfolk. At the age of eight he had been apprenticed by his parish overseers of the poor to William Iliff in Hinckley. After two years he ran away and joined the navy where he remained for eight years, presumably until he was eighteen years old. Joseph Throne, the 30 year old son of Sarah Throne, a Leicester single mother, was brought up in Burbage workhouse until he was about 12 or 13. The reason he was in Burbage workhouse was that Sarah had settlement there as she had been in service in the parish. He was

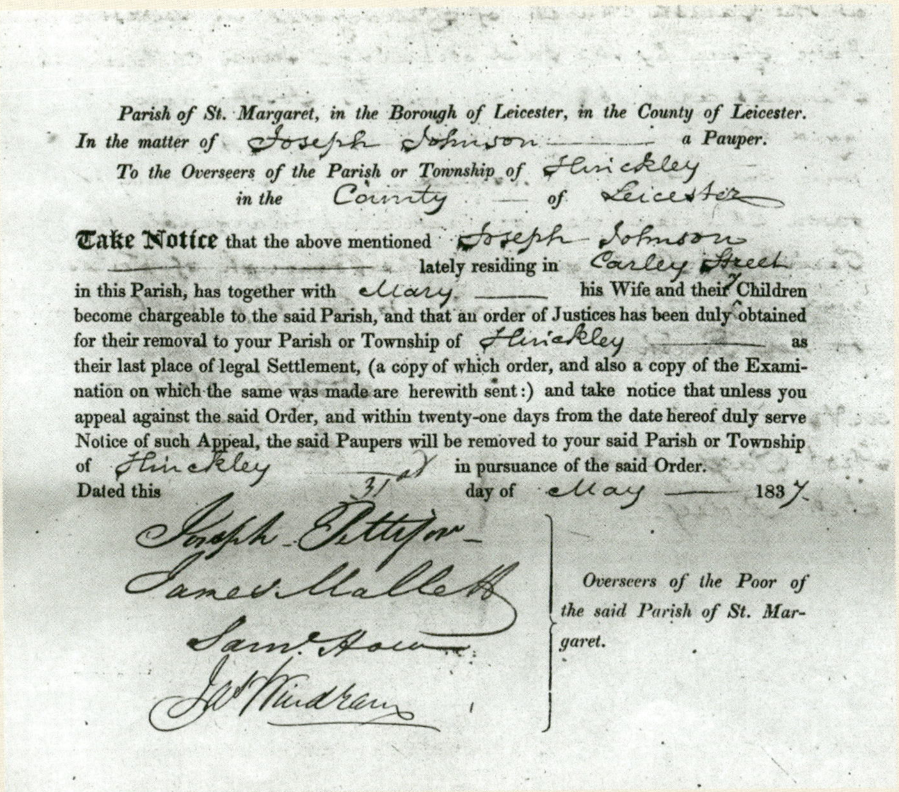

Parish of St. Margaret, in the Borough of Leicester, in the County of Leicester.
In the matter of Joseph Johnson *a Pauper.*
To the Overseers of the Parish or Township of Hinckley
in the County *of* Leicester

Take Notice that the above mentioned Joseph Johnson lately residing in Carley Street in this Parish, has together with Mary his Wife and their 7 Children become chargeable to the said Parish, and that an order of Justices has been duly obtained for their removal to your Parish or Township of Hinckley as their last place of legal Settlement, (a copy of which order, and also a copy of the Examination on which the same was made are herewith sent:) and take notice that unless you appeal against the said Order, and within twenty-one days from the date hereof duly serve Notice of such Appeal, the said Paupers will be removed to your said Parish or Township of Hinckley in pursuance of the said Order.
Dated this 31st day of May 1837.

Joseph Pettifor
James Mallett
Saml. Hall
Jno. Windram

Overseers of the Poor of the said Parish of St. Margaret.

Removal Order from St Margaret's Parish in Leicester to Hinckley for Josheph Johns on his wife and seven children

apprenticed by Burbage parish to John Brunt, a local framework knitter, but Brunt had died after only 14 months. Daniel Hands originally of Chilvers Coton in Warwickshire had been apprenticed to a Hinckley master called Beazley but ran away after 7 years to work as a journeyman in Leicester. Joseph Brown, born 45 years earlier in Coventry had been indentured to Daniel Allsop but ran away to enlist after four or five years. Thirty-five year old Stephen Lord had been born in Peckleton. The parish overseers had apprenticed him to Hinckley framework knitter, Thomas Williamson, at the age of 12. He served Williamson for two years but then had to leave for two years because he was short of work. He then returned and served for another five years. Lord had also tried his luck working in Thurlaston from where he had previously been removed back to Hinckley. Thomas Davenport had been born 41 years before in Monks Kirby, Warwickshire. He had been apprenticed to Thomas Showell but was released by the parish after just one and a half years because of his master's ill usage of him. He then found another place with Thomas Bassett. Edward Dickens born in Barwell, an old man of 76 had only been in Leicester for 6 months. He had been the keeper of a pub called the Pied Bull near the Angel in Islington and then a waiter. He had then been working as a journeyman stockingmaker for 20 years in Tewkesbury.

All these people who testified to the guardians of the poor in Leicester had been willing as adults to move in search of work to Leicester and even farther afield. As soon as there was a downward swing in the trade cycle, they were forced back to Hinckley as paupers once more to claim relief. Some of them testify that they had parents in Hinckley who were currently or had died in the workhouse there from whom they derive their settlement by nature of the father being apprenticed out as the child of paupers. Four generations of dire poverty are uncovered for those with dependent children by that one statement to the board of guardians. In the 1840's and again in the 1860's things were to become even worse.

From the descriptions of riots and unrest, people did not endure this suffering passively but collectively tried to solve their problems. Attempts to form trade unions were initially hampered by the domestic nature of the industry and the effect of the Combination Acts which outlawed most attempts at workers' organisation. In the 1820's a framework knitters' friendly society was formed to which members subscribed when they were in work in the belief they would receive payments when in need. Unfortunately this collapsed after just a few years because of the volume of claims made upon its funds by an impoverished membership.

The practice of taking on apprentices was obsolete by the time of the Commission of Inquiry into the Condition of Framework Knitters in the mid-1840's. This was because after the New Poor law Act in 1834, paying indenture fees for paupers put them at an advantage to non-paupers, the knitters' own children were the only source of child labour they could afford. Sadly, although the framework knitters were aware of the situation in their trade and would have liked their children to learn another, they could not afford the cost of the indenture fee for them to do so.

Panic on the streets: knitters protest at poverty pay!

The people of Hinckley did not endure their hardships passively. They did all they could to try and improve their situation, including trying to form unions, illegal under the Combination Acts, and friendly societies. Because of their poverty they could not afford regular subscriptions at a rate high enough to provide them with any benefits when so many needed to claim. All the framework knitters' organisations were short lived because of this. Other traditional forms of protest inherited from pre-industrial society were fallen back on as the only means available of drawing attention to their miserable, half-starving condition.

Sill's warehouse in Bond Street Hinckley was the scene of an assault on a Burbage man on 15 March 1826. The man was assailed by a number of people who ill-treated him and accused him of taking out work from the warehouse at an under price. A major employer, by the 1840's William Sill was employing over 800 knitters in and around the town (1). Mr Sill tried to intervene but received the same treatment himself. The angry group, described by the Leicester Chronicle as a mob, became uncontrollable and when he went for the magistrates and police Sill was abused further and injured by having a stone or brickbat thrown at him. In fury the windows and shutters of not only Sill's warehouse but those of other hosiers and shopkeepers were broken and destroyed causing about £200 worth of damage. Sill managed to escape through a shop in the Borough, got out of the back door and hid in a slaughter-house in the yard. Many other tradesmen such as publicans, shopkeepers and butchers gave out bread and money to the crowd in an attempt to purchase safety for themselves and their property. The protesters congregated outside Sill's house that evening. Mrs Sill fired a pistol at them through a window, an act that infuriated them so much they smashed every window in the place, before doing the same to every other hosiery manufacturer (2). The disturbance lasted for several hours, special constables were appointed and several arrests made (3).

The next day protesters broke into the Round House which was next to the Workhouse on the site of Council Road where some of those arrested were imprisoned. The prisoners were liberated when the prison doors were forced open with crowbars. The crowd then went to the Ram Inn which was on Castle Street. The inn was being used as an emergency gaol for the prisoners unable to fit in the Round House. Here again those in custody were set free by their neighbours. The collector of rates was at work in the town and he had his clothes torn from his back and his rate books seized and scattered in shreds (3). The gates of the Workhouse were torn down and burnt in the Market Place (4). A call was sent by the authorities for a company of lancers who after the riot act was read, escorted new prisoners arrested to Leicester Gaol which was more secure. Order had been restored, although later that week a farmhouse in Earl Shilton was raided by eight or nine people.

Reports of the incident used terms like "mob" and "rioters" to describe those taking part in the incident. These words convey an impression of mindlessness in the violence that ensued but if the targets of that violence are taken note of it can be seen that this violence was not mindless but clearly focused. The disturbance was sparked by the hosier, Sill, allegedly giving out work to an out-of-towner from Burbage to be completed at a lower rate of pay than that received by the Hinckley knitters. Undercutting of wage rates by village workers was a problem for town workers throughout the nineteenth century so this was unlikely to have been an isolated incident.

1 *First Appendix to the Report on the Condition of Framework Knitters, 1845, p252*
2 *Leicester Chronicle, 18 March 1826*
3 *Hinckley Parish Magazine, November 1873, p42*
4 *Hinckley Parish Magazine, November 1873, p43*
5 *Francis, History of Hinckley, p128*

Undercutting not only reduced the amount of work available for town people but depressed rates of pay as well, so the Hinckley people had a valid grievance with the hosiers who failed to pay the correct rate to poor villagers probably desperately poor themselves. Because of the domestic nature of the framework knitting industry it was difficult for the workers to organise themselves in a union to protest through strike action, besides they were too poor to pay a subscription out of their meagre wages. Attempts to form friendly societies failed because of this poverty, more money would have to be paid out than the members could possible pay in. The poor stockingers would also not have been entitled to vote as they would not have met the property qualification. They had no legitimate means of making their anger known and no alternative way of protesting. Collective bargaining by riot was a common feature of pre-industrial protest and was seen as perfectly legitimate by those participating who felt that the masters were the ones in the wrong. The masters were breaking the moral economy by depriving them of work, food and access to the land which might have enabled them to eke out a subsistence. Reports in local newspapers of convictions of Hinckley people for trespass and poaching on the land of the wealthy are common throughout the nineteenth century.

There had been rioting in Hinckley before. In a series of articles on the History of Hinckley in the parish magazine for 1873 earlier instances are described, one of which took place in the late eighteenth and early nineteenth centuries. Combined with a depression in trade and consequent low earnings, the price of bread was extremely high. The knitters held discussions about the situation and the employers were very unpopular. Rumours were also circulating of new machinery, which if introduced, would deprive them of their livelihood. Threats were made against the masters, some of whom put watchmen on their warehouses. "The men felt annoyed seeing the warehouses closed against them, their frames unemployed, and the yarn stored up while they were starving" (6). The people were starving; there was no bread, the staple food at the time and potatoes were just about all they had to live on. Pressure was building up. The knitters claimed the right to work the masters' machinery and yarn. Believing the masters were keeping them unemployed unnecessarily, on Easter Monday while the Fair was being held, they set to work. A cheering crowd paraded round the town with a black flag and some loaves dipped in blood. The manufacturers had closed the warehouses for the afternoon because of the fair. The crowd smashed warehouse windows and threw goods into the street. They also got into one of the employer's homes and smashed up his furniture. The crowd then sacked Wykin Hall of its cheese, butter, wheat and other food items. They were not thieves and saw themselves acting to promote justice. The pillaged food was taken to Hinckley market and disposed of at such prices as they thought reasonable. The disturbances were stopped when the Leicestershire Yeomanry Cavalry came to the scene. The captured ringleaders when brought to trial were ordered to give the money taken in the sale to the original owner of the foodstuffs. Nothing else was done to them, the authorities perhaps being anxious to avoid further trouble. At this time house breaking was common also because the townspeople believed that farmers deliberately withheld supplies to get higher prices. The richer classes were very unpopular and, according to the parish magazine, on one occasion a donkey's head was cut off (from a supposed similarity between the word ass and aristocrat), crowned and set up on a post (7).

Trade was again very bad in 1811 and once more pauperism and want became the norm for the knitters and their families. They began to organise together in order to secure an increase in the rates of pay and determined to destroy any kind of machinery which would lessen manual labour. Distress was blamed on the introduction of wide frames which could make several stockings at once which were not fully-fashioned but cut-ups. According to the Parish Magazine these Luddites, in disguise, prowled about at midnight for the purposes of destroying these machines and succeeded in doing a vast amount of damage. Secret meetings with delegates from other areas were held at night (8). This sounds quite sinister but it must be remembered that the Combination Acts forbade workers' from organising openly. The Parish Magazine implied that Luddites were responsible for the disturbance of 1811 and that discontent focussed on the introduction of new machinery. There is little evidence of new machinery or of its destruction in Hinckley at that time. The knitters were concerned with declining wages and high food prices, not the machines themselves. Throughout the East Midlands hosiery producing area in 1811-12 there was discontent with low pay. When machines were smashed it was a tactic to ensure solidarity in strikes for groups of workers who were too poor to create a fund for strike pay and it was used in the Nottingham area as part of a struggle for a living wage in conjunction with negotiation (9). There was no better way, in a domestic based industry scattered through a town or in several villages, that scabbing could be effectively prevented. Machine breaking was just another tactic not an end in itself. An Elmesthorpe farmer, Richard Fowkes kept a diary which in 1874 was read to the Leicestershire Archaeological Society by the vicar of Earl Shilton, Rev Tower. Fowkes makes no mention of Luddism or machine breaking. Two entries for April 1811 describe the desperation of the stocking makers against a background of national events and how they expressed it. The entry for 2 April said "The news of the day is the English beat 8,000 French with 3,000 men". It seems that the poor people of Hinckley had nothing to celebrate in this news, even though many men had enlisted. On 5 April, Fowkes wrote "This day is called Old Lady Day, though by the almanack 'tis a day later. A half-year's Rent-day which for many people comes too soon before the Rent is ready". This statement does not relate specifically to stocking makers who nonetheless would have suffered by agricultural problems because of the general effect on the prices of food and payment given for their work. On the 8 April the diary said "Riots by the stocking-makers of Hinckley about the prices. On Saturday night (ie 6 April 1811) breaking windows, plundering and burning and pulling down houses" (10).

---

6 *Hinckley Parish Magazine, November, 1873, p39-40*

7 *Hinckley Parish Magazine, 1873; Francis, History of Hinckley, p127*

8 *Hinckley Parish Magazine, p 40*

10 *Transactions of the Leicestershire Archaeological Society, Volume IV, p296.*

The incidents of April 1826 were a continuation of traditional forms of protest although now they had a more industrial focus as England was transforming from a mainly agrarian to an industrial economy. As well as hosiers being the targets of the crowd, shopkeepers, inn keepers and butchers also felt the need to placate the crowd to avoid attacks on their property. The system of frame rents often paid to people in trades not directly connected to hosiery who merely wanted an investment and the truck system would have made these people as unpopular as the employers. It also matches the events of earlier riots where the desperate protesters were re-appropriating food from the rich to themselves. The rate collector was a symbol of authority from a system that didn't seem to care much for them and whose Poor Law provided inadequately for the poor. The Workhouse was targeted because it was symbolic of oppression and a system that punished the poor for their own poverty. Liberating the prisoners indicates that the crowd thought that they had moral authority for their actions and that the authorities had no right to punish the perpetrators.

Those arrested were treated relatively leniently by the court in Leicester on 8 April 1826. A young man, William Robinson was indicted for riot on 15 March. In evidence against him the constable, Benjamin Pearson, said that he saw Robinson, who was with a group of stone throwers, pick up a stone. The court found him guilty despite the accused's assertion that he only picked up the stone as a joke and would not really have thrown it. Due to the mitigating factor of the obvious distress in the area Robinson was sentenced to three months hard labour, a relatively light sentence for that kind of offence in those days. Another youth, John Bagworth, received the same sentence for the same charge. Richard Duddle was sentenced to two months hard labour and a fourth youth, Charles Paul, was acquitted . All the youths arrested were between the ages of 16 and 18 years and were of good character Leicester Chronicle, 8 April 1826.

The distress in Hinckley was beginning to affect the middle classes and not just the knitters. The Poor Rates were costing them £1 a week. No work meant that there was no money to spend and so shopkeepers were also deprived of customers, even for truck. The Hinckley Commercial Bank collapsed and along with it the fortunes of Mr Sansome who was part of another local bank. The riot was not a futile act because it brought to the attention of the outside world the plight of the impoverished framework knitters. In May 1826 £200 was sent to help them avoid starvation by the London Relief Committee.

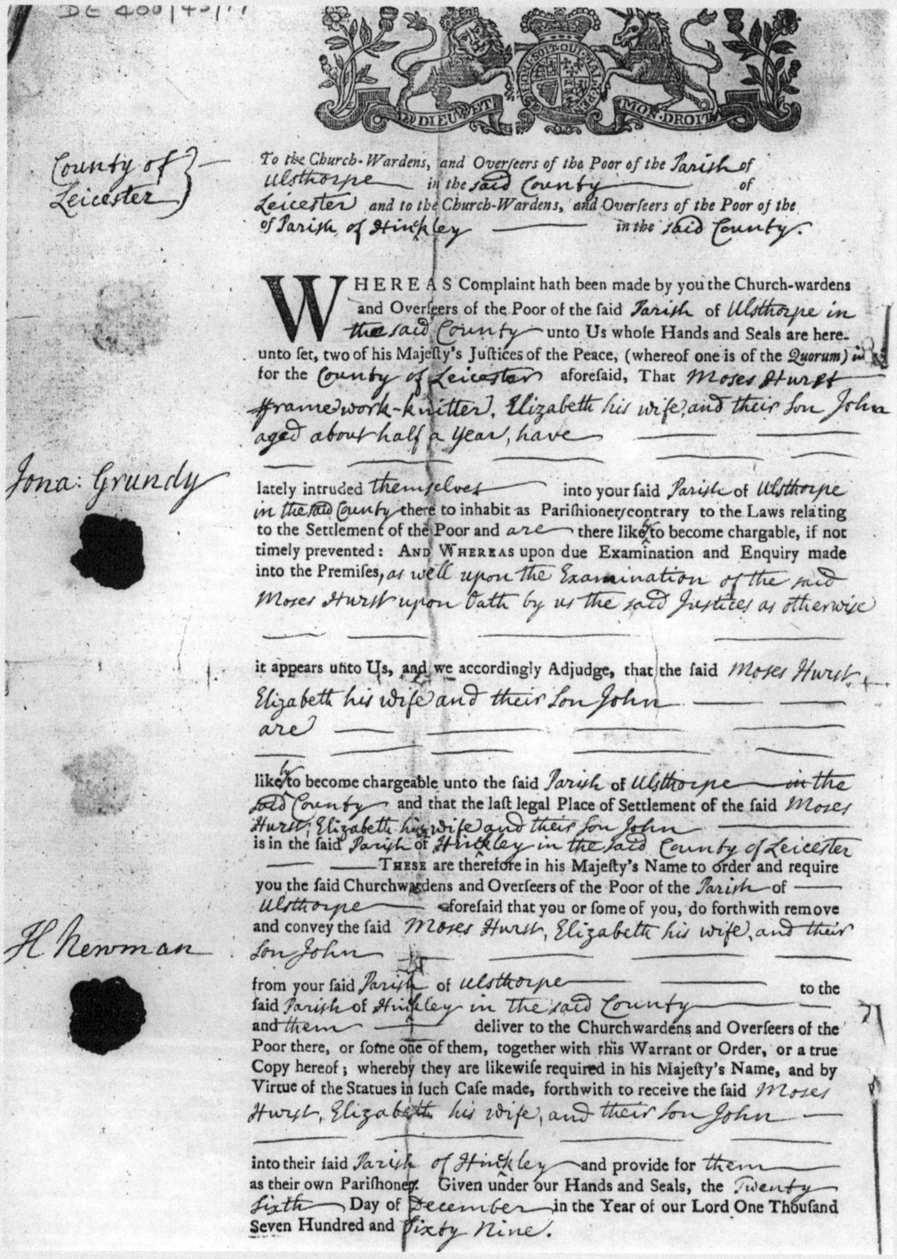
County of Leicester } To the Church-Wardens, and Overseers of the Poor of the Parish of Ulsthorpe in the said County of Leicester and to the Church-Wardens, and Overseers of the Poor of the Parish of Hinckley in the said County.

WHEREAS Complaint hath been made by you the Church-wardens and Overseers of the Poor of the said Parish of Ulsthorpe in the said County unto Us whose Hands and Seals are hereunto set, two of his Majesty's Justices of the Peace, (whereof one is of the Quorum) in for the County of Leicester aforesaid, That Moses Hurst Framework-knitter, Elizabeth his wife, and their son John aged about half a Year, have lately intruded themselves into your said Parish of Ulsthorpe in the said County there to inhabit as Parishioners contrary to the Laws relating to the Settlement of the Poor and are there likely to become chargable, if not timely prevented: And Whereas upon due Examination and Enquiry made into the Premises, as well upon the Examination of the said Moses Hurst upon Oath by us the said Justices as otherwise it appears unto Us, and we accordingly Adjudge, that the said Moses Hurst, Elizabeth his wife and their son John are likely to become chargeable unto the said Parish of Ulsthorpe in the said County and that the last legal Place of Settlement of the said Moses Hurst, Elizabeth his wife and their son John is in the said Parish of Hinckley in the said County of Leicester. These are therefore in his Majesty's Name to order and require you the said Churchwardens and Overseers of the Poor of the Parish of Ulsthorpe aforesaid that you or some of you, do forthwith remove and convey the said Moses Hurst, Elizabeth his wife, and their son John from your said Parish of Ulsthorpe to the said Parish of Hinckley in the said County and them deliver to the Churchwardens and Overseers of the Poor there, or some one of them, together with this Warrant or Order, or a true Copy hereof; whereby they are likewise required in his Majesty's Name, and by Virtue of the Statues in such Case made, forthwith to receive the said Moses Hurst, Elizabeth his wife, and their son John into their said Parish of Hinckley and provide for them as their own Parishoner. Given under our Hands and Seals, the Twenty sixth Day of December in the Year of our Lord One Thousand Seven Hundred and Sixty Nine.

Jona: Grundy

H Newman

Hungry Hinckley

The 1840's in England is a period that has been described and remembered as the "Hungry Forties" because of economic depression. Hinckley suffered as much as any of the worst affected areas, but it was not just the "Hungry Forties" in the town but hungry twenties, thirties, forties and later, eighteen-sixties too. Until the mid-1830's framework knitters without enough work had been able to go to Leicester in search of work in the woollen branch of the trade but that source of employment also stagnated as the price of wool plummeted. Out of work Hinckley knitters who had moved to Leicester were being removed under the orders of the Guardians of the Poor back to their "parish of settlement" even if they had moved away many years earlier and had settled down in the larger town. They were deemed to be dependent on relief from Hinckley parish even if they had very little to do with the town. In 1837 it was estimated that about 3,000 people in Hinckley were dependent on Parish Relief. This was out of a population of around 6,475, with only about 450 ratepayers! The poor-rates rose to 4s 2d in the pound in 1842 for one quarter alone. The New Poor Laws of 1834 made the qualification for relief and the level of assistance received much more stringent. The able-bodied poor were supposed to go into the workhouse to receive a standard of living much lower than they could expect by working as a detriment to supposed idleness and to distinguish between the "deserving" and "undeserving" poor. The guardians had much less discretion about what kind of help a person or family might receive than previously even where they had sympathy for the claimant's case. Guardians were bound to exercise the strictest economy when allocating relief even when that relief was hardly enough to keep the recipients from starving. The New Poor Law's application had practically broken down in Hinckley. The workhouse was full and so it was not possible to give indoor relief to all the needy families, perhaps luckily so when the conditions inside the workhouse are considered. Inside families were broken up because of the policy of sexual segregation, paupers as they were styled had to wear a uniform and all were subject to a very strict regime as well as having to work at laborious menial tasks. Relief in the town was given half in bread and half in money. For a family this was worth about a shilling a head, for instance for a man, his wife and two children the amount paid out was 2 shillings in cash and four loaves of bread, also worth 2 shillings. Out of this all out-goings had to be met, such as rent, fuel for heating and lighting, soap, clothing and food other than bread.

Self-help schemes, like the Framework Knitters' Friendly Society started through the efforts of Robert Hall, were all failures owing to the poverty of the membership who could not afford to pay an adequate, regular subscription and the terrific drain on resources caused by the numbers needing to claim out of work benefits. During the period between 1839 and 1841, 13 out of 15 sick clubs in Hinckley, with about 1,000 members between them, closed because the members could not afford the subscriptions .

To alleviate the situation a benevolent scheme was proposed, to which better off individuals could subscribe. This fund could then be used to mitigate some of the worst cases of suffering and distress. An address to the inhabitants of Hinckley calling for this proposal to be put into action was circulated on 2 June 1837 by J S Needham, J H Small, Robert Heathcoat, Samuel Bonner and James Hollier. In it they outlined the situation in the town regarding poverty and the limitations of the New Poor Law and proposed to set up a fund whereby private subscriptions could be dispensed to the very poorest by a committee. No matter how generous the subscribers, though, it would not have been possible for half the community to be dependent on the other for subsistence through the Poor Rates and charity. The Poor Rates escalated and local shop keepers and traders as well as those dependent on

1 *This has been calculated as an approximate mid-point between the figures for 1831 and 1841 as given by William Biggs in his address to the manufacturers of the Midlands in 1841*

2 *Hinckley Parish Magazine, November 1873, p46*

3 *Victoria County History, Leicestershire, Volume III, p14*

knitting were also facing a decline in their income as well as the increased financial burden of supporting so many of their poor and half-starved neighbours.

Things did not improve at all over the next decade. In 1841 Derby hosted a convention of around 400 representatives of the Midlands manufacturing community. From the report of their discussions, politically these middle-class employers were radicals and supporters of the call for the repeal of the Corn Laws. They were opposed to the Tory party that under Sir Robert Peel defeated the liberal Whigs later that year amidst the country's deepening economic troubles. Peel himself was not a hard-line Conservative and increasingly became associated with free-trade and the demand for the Corn Laws' repeal which he implemented in 1846 in the confused political aftermath of the catastrophe in Ireland of the potato famine. An extract from the speech made by Leicester hosiery manufacturer, political radical, social reformer, councillor and some-time mayor, William Biggs, is quoted at length here. Biggs' hosiery firm, John Biggs and Son of Leicester, put out work in Hinckley and some of the surrounding villages. Biggs' speech gives a very clear picture of the situation regarding the extreme poverty in Hinckley without becoming sentimental. The facts related by him speak for themselves.

"The population of Hinckley in 1831 was 6,491 - in 1841 it was 6,459; shewing a diminution which though trifling, is anything but an index of prosperity. The poor-rates for 1815 were £2,929; for 1841 they are £4,240. Between which times it must be recollected the population remained nearly stationary in amount. In 1811 there were twenty-five houses unoccupied; in 1831 there were 122; and in 1841 there were 157: - thus showing an increase of deserted tenements, and evidencing a gradual and growing pauperism among the working classes. In the year 1815, the clear earnings of an average workman were 12 shillings per week; in the year 1841, when fully employed, they would not exceed from seven shillings to eight shillings, but for the last three years, the workmen have not been fully employed, even at this reduced rate. Those engaged in the manufacture of brown cotton hosiery (which is the principle article and chief support of Hinckley) have been unemployed for fully one third of their time for the last three years, and the deficiency of employment has gone on greatly increasing during the same period"(4).

"Of those who are in work, one-half only are fully employed, the other half being limited to what is called half-work, which does not exceed in amount four shillings per week. This, it must be understood, has occurred in a town, in a manufacture, where not the slightest alteration or improvement of machinery has taken place; so that of course the distress and reduction of wages here cannot, by possibility, be ascribed to machinery, as steam power has never been employed, in Hinckley or its neighbourhood, in the manufacture of cotton hosiery; but the distress, as evidenced by the poor-rates, can be distinctly proved to be greater in years when corn is dear, than in other years when corn is cheap; as for instance in 1835, when corn was 39s 4d per quarter, the poor-rates amounted to £2,010 - in 1836, when corn was 48s 6d per quarter, they amounted to £2,070 - in 1840, after three consecutive dear years, and when corn was 66s 4d per quarter they amounted to £3,120 - and now in 1841, when corn is 64s 6d per quarter, they amount to £4,240. From which coincidences we are warranted in believing, as practical men, that dear corn has a natural tendency to produce bad trade, reduction of wages and general distress. Frame property has depreciated in Hinckley to a great extent; it is not possible to say precisely to what extent, as frames are not now vendible by auction at any price. The last sale was stopped, after the first few frames were disposed of; and those which were sold did not realize much more than half the valuation. In 1815 the average value of frames, as attested by sales at public

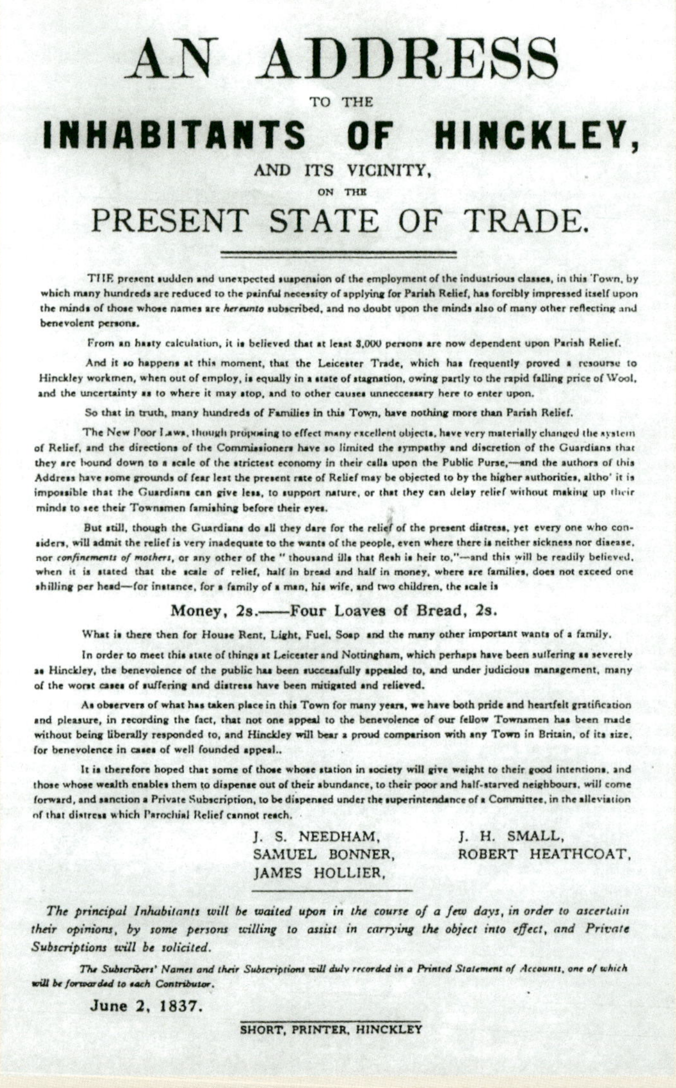
AN ADDRESS

TO THE

INHABITANTS OF HINCKLEY,

AND ITS VICINITY,

ON THE

PRESENT STATE OF TRADE.

THE present sudden and unexpected suspension of the employment of the industrious classes, in this Town, by which many hundreds are reduced to the painful necessity of applying for Parish Relief, has forcibly impressed itself upon the minds of those whose names are *hereunto* subscribed, and no doubt upon the minds also of many other reflecting and benevolent persons.

From an hasty calculation, it is believed that at least 3,000 persons are now dependent upon Parish Relief.

And it so happens at this moment, that the Leicester Trade, which has frequently proved a resourse to Hinckley workmen, when out of employ, is equally in a state of stagnation, owing partly to the rapid falling price of Wool, and the uncertainty as to where it may stop, and to other causes unneccessary here to enter upon.

So that in truth, many hundreds of Families in this Town, have nothing more than Parish Relief.

The New Poor Laws, though proposing to effect many excellent objects, have very materially changed the system of Relief, and the directions of the Commissioners have so limited the sympathy and discretion of the Guardians that they are bound down to a scale of the strictest economy in their calls upon the Public Purse,—and the authors of this Address have some grounds of fear lest the present rate of Relief may be objected to by the higher authorities, altho' it is impossible that the Guardians can give less, to support nature, or that they can delay relief without making up their minds to see their Townsmen famishing before their eyes.

But still, though the Guardians do all they dare for the relief of the present distress, yet every one who considers, will admit the relief is very inadequate to the wants of the people, even where there is neither sickness nor disease, nor *confinements of mothers*, or any other of the " thousand ills that flesh is heir to,"—and this will be readily believed, when it is stated that the scale of relief, half in bread and half in money, where are families, does not exceed one shilling per head—for instance, for a family of a man, his wife, and two children, the scale is

Money, 2s.——Four Loaves of Bread, 2s.

What is there then for House Rent, Light, Fuel, Soap and the many other important wants of a family.

In order to meet this state of things at Leicester and Nottingham, which perhaps have been suffering as severely as Hinckley, the benevolence of the public has been successfully appealed to, and under judicious management, many of the worst cases of suffering and distress have been mitigated and relieved.

As observers of what has taken place in this Town for many years, we have both pride and heartfelt gratification and pleasure, in recording the fact, that not one appeal to the benevolence of our fellow Townsmen has been made without being liberally responded to, and Hinckley will bear a proud comparison with any Town in Britain, of its size, for benevolence in cases of well founded appeal..

It is therefore hoped that some of those whose station in society will give weight to their good intentions, and those whose wealth enables them to dispense out of their abundance, to their poor and half-starved neighbours, will come forward, and sanction a Private Subscription, to be dispensed under the superintendance of a Committee, in the alleviation of that distress which Parochial Relief cannot reach.

J. S. NEEDHAM, J. H. SMALL,
SAMUEL BONNER, ROBERT HEATHCOAT,
JAMES HOLLIER,

The principal Inhabitants will be waited upon in the course of a few days, in order to ascertain their opinions, by some persons willing to assist in carrying the object into effect, and Private Subscriptions will be solicited.

The Subscribers' Names and their Subscriptions will duly recorded in a Printed Statement of Accounts, one of which will be forwarded to each Contributor.

June 2, 1837.

SHORT, PRINTER, HINCKLEY

Broadsheet calling for Relief Fund to help the poor.

4 *William Biggs' speech, Commercial Distress Convention of the Manufacturers of the Midland Counties, Derby, Thursday December 9, 1841, found in William Biggs' Scrapbook which is in Leics Records Office (LRO), Acc no 5D61/1*

No Work, No Bread, No Hope!

A

MEETING

OF THE

INHABITANTS OF HINCKLEY

WILL BE HELD

NEAR THE HOLY WELL,

ON TUESDAY EVENING, JUNE 28, 1842,

AT SEVEN O'CLOCK:

To consider and to adopt such Resolutions as are required by the present times, in which the Hosier has little Trade and no Profit; the Landlord no Rent; the Shop-keeper no Custom; the Stockinger neither Bread nor Hope; and in which the heavy Poor-Rates are involving the Householder and the neighbouring Farmer in one Common Ruin.

Hinckley, June 22, 1842.

BURGESS, PRINTER, HINCKLEY.

auction, was £8 14s - in 1826 and 1827 they were depreciated to £6 3s 6d - in 1840 to £4 1s., at present, in 1841, there is no price for them. It is necessary of course to say, that the value of frames is regulated by the profitable or unprofitable nature of the business. Hinckley and the villages adjoining, contain one-fifth of the frames in Leicestershire, and were principally dependent on the American market for employment. Hinckley goods are now beaten out of the United States market by the manufacturers from the Continent. The articles in which we have been superseded by the Germans are; men's and women's brown and coloured hose and half-hose. The prospects for Hinckley are gloomy in the extreme; the declared intentions of some of the largest manufacturers are, to sell their machinery and get out of the trade, owing to the absence of all profit in carrying it on for the last few years, and the ruinous depreciation in the value of manufactured goods. In several cases of insolvency in this town and neighbourhood, it has been found that goods have been repeatedly sold, for the last three years at ruinous sacrifice at a loss of at least from fifteen to twenty-five per cent. The demand for labour seems to decrease here more and more every year, and in the same proportion the comforts and respectability of the working-classes decrease with it; and all the exertions of religious teachers of Sunday schools cannot and do not retard the rapid progress of demoralization which is, in consequence, fearfully extending itself. Hunger and distress are fast destroying all honestly in our sex, and all chastity and decency in the other. As painfully interesting evidence of the extreme state of poverty to which the operatives are reduced, it is a fact, that thirteen out of fifteen sick clubs or friendly societies, in this town are shut up, from the inability of their members to pay the subscriptions; and some intention has been entertained of dividing up the funds, and breaking up the clubs altogether. Here is poverty, destitution, and despair..."

"One-third of the frames and workmen at Hinckley are at the present time totally unemployed; one-third only earning from seven shillings to eight shillings per week; and the remaining one-third employed upon half work, by which they can earn only four shillings per week. It has been found to be impossible to carry out all the provisions of the New Poor Law into operation in Hinckley. It has been repeatedly tried but has regularly failed. Last year (1840) there were 500 men, heads of families, out of the small population of Hinckley parish, in the workhouse yard breaking stones; this year the poor-house is full, and the unemployed poor, who are not in the house, are necessarily relieved out of it. The poor-rates, which used to be, in a healthy state of the trade, 10d in the pound per quarter, or £3 4d per year, are now 20d per quarter, or £6 8d per year; being in other words, double what they formerly were, with no prospect of alteration or reduction. The state of destitution here is attended with wretchedness which will not bear description; it is too bad to be portrayed and is too extensive to be relieved".

A slight improvement to the condition of some of the stockingers came about by the introduction of allotments in about 1842. Nearly 40 acres of land were placed at their disposal and let to them at low rent. A select committee in the House of Commons had looked at the benefits to be gained from these allotments. Hinckley witnesses to this committee showed that something had to be done to help the pauperised knitters. These allotments helped the holders to grow extra provisions for their families in a year when between 25 March and 21 June, 2,457 people out of a population of 6,450 claimed poor relief Hinckley (5). Each year Lord Howe gave £10 as prizes to the best cultivators.

5 *Parish Magazine, November 1873, p47*

To the GENTLEMEN, TRADESMEN, and PUBLIC at large, of HINCKLEY, and its Vicinity.

IT is a generally admitted truth that "union is strength," hence the Divine Proverb "a three-fold cord is not easily broken." It is true, power may be used as an instrument either for good or evil, either to enslave or set free. The tyranny of the mob as well as the crown despot is alike hateful and intolerable. There is no man over whose mind reason has asserted its right who pants to be crushed beneath the oppressors power, to writhe under his scorpion rod. To bring then, into operation a balancing power to regulate the social position of masters and men would indeed be a desideratum advantageous to both parties alike, but this can only be done by fraternity and union. The various benevolent Associations which are the ornament and glory of the British Nation, each has one special object in view, and without these combinations nothing can be more clear that none of these objects would be obtained by individual effort; and we feel no hesitation in saying that the Framework-knitters will never rise to occupy that station in civil society which is so very desirable unless they as a body become united. With regard to what is so often said about supply and demand regulating wages, we hold all such stupid cant in sovereign contempt—and the mercenary scribes too who make use of such language—with the view to gull poor men into the belief that the adoption of remedial plans are futile and unnecessary! Why, we know very well, in times of depression, our wages fall fast enough, but in seasons of briskness they do not always rise.

It is notorious that a few months back the demand exceeded the supply, and yet a desperate struggle took place ere a small advance could be obtained. Facts are stubborn things—are far more convincing than flimsy arguments. The time is now come, we conceive, when attempts at least ought to be made to unite the whole Stocking Trade, comprehending the whole of our village population, for without their co-operation nothing effectually can be done. We recommend that separate Unions be formed in each Town and Village, that the funds be under the control of a Committee, composed of Tradesmen, that they be held morally responsible for the carrying out of the legitimate objects of the Society.—viz. Protection to the Fair Tradesman—Upholding the Rights of Labour—and the Suppression of the Truck.

To our fellow-workmen we advisedly say, now is the period for a resolute persevering effort, to free yourselves from that galling yoke you have worn so long. You are degraded and miserable.—Why should you be so? Has the God of Providence decreed it?—By no means. Why, your situation ought to be such as to enable you, with the exercise of frugality and economy, to hoard up a little against a "rainy day." If your circumstances do not improve now, your prospects are truly gloomy; your Sick Clubs are insolvent, some of them defunct, and should afflictions arise you have nothing before you but the Union House. Who, we demand, that has any feelings of self respect, any manly pride, any spirit of independence, but dreads the idea of being burdensome to others even as much as death itself.

The Inhabitants of Hinckley have long groaned under the pressure of enormous Poor-Rates, and some of our thrifty Shop-keepers have been nearly ruined. The Framework-knitters themselves have become a proverb and a by-word in the nation. Let them one and all unite to make a long pull, a strong pull, and a pull together, in order to bring about a better and happier state of things.

We have much pleasure in stating that J. BROWN, ESQ. has kindly accepted the office of Treasurer, and as Nottingham, Leicester and other places, are making strenuous efforts to better the condition of the Framework-knitters, we once more solicit your aid to carry out the objects embodied in this bill. Proper persons will shortly be appointed to solicit Subscriptions.

Signed on behalf of the Trade,

Wide Branch.

WILLIAM CROFTS.
GEORGE WOODWARD.
THOMAS FREER.

JOHN GINNS, Secretary.

Wrought Branch.

WILLIAM HACKETT.
WILLIAM BURTON.
JAMES SPIERS.
JOHN SILVESTER.
THOMAS CLEWS.

JAMES PRATT, Secretary.

Short Printer, Hinckley

JABEZ CHAPLIN, Chairman.

Concern at the condition of the framework knitters led to political interest and to the government sponsored hosiery commission inquiry which reported on evidence given before it, published in 1845. Felkin, one of the members of this commission, made a report outlining some of the evidence reported to him on the state of the trade in 1844. In it he described each of the hosiery producing towns and villages in the East Midlands; he did not find one good thing to say regarding the physical and economic condition of the framework knitters in these villages. Of Burbage, where cotton hose was chiefly made, he said that the hands were in miserable circumstances with clear earnings of 5s 6d. In Barwell, the work was nearly all cotton-hose. People were better off than in some places. Although earnings were not much more most families could cultivate large plots of ground paying only a nominal rent. Cotton hose was again the chief manufacture of Earl Shilton. The framework knitters there were so very poor and the wages received so low that it was claimed workhouse pay and fare was a preferable condition. In Stoke Golding worsted hosiery was made with yarn given out by bag or middlemen. Much distress prevailed there while in nearby Dadlington the few framework knitters living there lived in houses on waste land and were paid a mere acknowledgement. In the town of Hinckley itself, the earnings were stated by several hosiers to be 5s 3d a week. The agent reporting on the state of those in the trade there agreed

THE ADDRESS

OF THE

HINCKLEY FRAMEWORK-KNITTERS,

TO THE PUBLIC IN GENERAL.

"Blessed is he that Considereth the Poor."

The season of the year being now at hand when the great mercantile houses of London engaged in the Hosiery Trade send their Agents into this our Market, who commonly make large contracts for Manufactured Goods, and as a necessary consequence, buy up the labour of the Framework-knitters for long periods to *come;* we feel ourselves compelled by stern necessity, arising out of our duty to our wives and families, to address you at this momentous time, with a cold, dark, and dreary *Winter* before us, and *famine* around us, owing to the failure of those crops by which the poor are principally sustained, and the unparalleled low rate of wages paid in this district. In adopting this method, in order to place our real position before the public eye: we utterly disclaim having any intention or wish to disturb that harmony and good will, which ever ought to exist between masters and men; but, common justice demands that the situation of the Framework-knitters of this town and its vicinity, should be fully known and understood. Could we assure ourselves that our present low prices were necessary, we would endeavour to be resigned to the hardness of our lot. Could it be shown that our sufferings were consistent with the arrangements of Divine Providence, submission would then become our duty. Did we believe that a small advance would militate against the interests of our employers or the community, we would not ask for it. We will not offer an opinion of our *own* upon this subject, well knowing that the judgment of an interested party, would weigh but little with wise and discerning men.

We have repeatedly appealed to our employers during the last three years, (since the demand for our labour has been so abundant,) for a small advance of wages, and we have as often been told by a great majority of them "*that our requests were reasonable, that they were willing to give it, and that the state of the markets would justify it:*" but it has never been REALIZED.

Recently, it has been recommended to make an effort to raise the prices of the Framework-knitters in Nottinghamshire, thereby intimating that then a way would be opened for an advance here. A letter was therefore instantly dispatched to a first-rate house of Nottingham, soliciting information relative to the rate of wages paid by *them;* the following reply has been received, which we have the pleasure of laying before the public; the writer is a gentleman of high standing, of unblemished reputation, and of unimpeachable veracity; the extracts are as follows:—

Nottingham, September 24th, 1845.

Sir,

*I received your letter and cannot but feel compassion for the Framework-knitters of your Town and Neighbourhood. We make no Cotton Stockings, in Nottinghamshire, lower than 24 gages, and therefore your Manufacturers meet with no competition from us, or I believe from any other Manufacturers in 22 gages and under; I do not see therefore but they might advance the prices of those low gages. We charge 9d. per week rent for all narrow frames up to 30 gage, all above 1s. All sorts are narrowed two plain in the gusset, that is, shift four stitches and narrow two; every other part is narrowed one plain, that is, shift three stitches and narrow two, except some finer sorts, which are narrowed two plain throughout, these are paid 1s. per dozen extra.**

Mr. James Leigh.

The following scale presents a comparative view of the prices paid at Nottingham and Hinckley and its Vicinity.

NOTTINGHAM.

Gage.		Jacks.	Length.	Price.	
30	hose		26½	10	0
30	half hose	102	11½	5	0
26	hose	124	26½	8	9
26	half hose	86	11½	4	3
24	hose	114	26½	7	9
24	half hose	82	11½	3	9

6 jacks wider, leg 1 inch longer, 6*d.* extra.

N.B. Some Hosiers give 3*d.* more for the half hose but they may be set on a lead or two wider. All sorts named are narrowed 1 plain, except the gusset. The Nottingham Framework-knitter pays 9*d.* per week for his frame.

HINCKLEY.

Gage.		Jacks.	Length.	Price.	
30	hose	125	24	7	3
30	half hose	98	12½	4	9
26	hose	121	27	7	9
26	half hose	86	12	4	0
24	hose	111	27	7	0
24	half hose	77 to 79	12½	3	0

N.B. All these sorts are narrowed 2 plain, with the exception of the 24 gage half hose, which have no narrowings in the gusset. The Hinckley Framework-knitter commonly working inferior yarn, which is often equal to a loss of 5 per cent upon his earnings, and is charged 1*s.* and sometimes more for his frame.

These are facts which no man living can disprove; where then is the "*Competition from Nottingham*", or any other place? all we ask is to be put upon a par with the wrought-hose Framework-knitters of that town; were this the case, and were our different sorts of work paid in the same proportion, and the same amount of rent charged for the frames, there would be an increased circulation of at least £.75 per week, or £.3,750 per annum, in Hinckley alone.

JAMES LEIGH,
THOMAS BROOKS,
THOMAS ALSOP.

* The original is in our possession, and may be seen by any one who may doubt the statements set forth in this address.

HINCKLEY, October 18, 1845.

Lee, Printer, Hinckley.

with this figure and added that the condition of the frame work knitters was so deplorably bad as to beggar all description, but many local people were prepared to describe it and examples of the deep poverty and utter deprivation and despair for the future were given in evidence to the Commissioners in their inquiry. Despite the low wages, knitters had to pay frame-rent of between 1s and 2s a week out of these meagre earnings. It was calculated that one shilling and one and a half pence each a week was all that was left to the families of 1,600 framework knitters in the town with which to pay for rent, food, clothing, fire and other necessities (6).

Descriptions of life for framework knitters can be found in the Report on the Condition of the Framework Knitters of 1845, the First Report of the Royal Commission on the State of Large Towns and Populous Districts of 1843.

Yet again, 1845 was a terrible year for the framework knitters. Not because of unemployment this time but because of low pay and high prices. As part of a campaign for an increase in rates of pay, an address given on behalf of the Hinckley framework knitters to the public in general was headed "Blessed is he that Considereth the Poor". The address began "the season of the year being now at hand when the great mercantile houses of London engaged in the Hosiery Trade send their Agents into this our Market, who commonly make large contracts for Manufactured Goods, and as a necessary consequence, buy up the labour of the Framework-knitters for long periods to come; we feel ourselves compelled by stern necessity, arising out of our duty to our wives and families, to address you at this momentous time, with a cold, dark, and dreary Winter before us and famine around us, owing to the failure of those crops by which the poor are principally sustained, and the unparalleled low rate of wages paid in this district. In adopting this method, in order to place our real position before the public eye: we utterly disclaim having any intention or wish to disturb that harmony and good will, which ever ought to exist between masters and men; but, common justice

6 *W Felkin, An Account of machine-wrought Hosiery Trade: its extent and the condition of the framework-knitters: a peeper read in the statistical section, at the second York meeting of British Association held september 18, 1844 together with the evidence given under the Hosiery Commission Inquirey, London, 1845.*

demands that the situation of the Framework-knitters of this town and its vicinity, should be fully known and understood. Could we assure ourselves that our present low prices were necessary, we would endeavour to be resigned to the hardness of our lot. Could it be shown that our sufferings were consistent with the arrangements of Divine Providence, submission would then become our duty. Did we believe that a small advance would militate against the interests of our employers or the community, we would not ask for it. We will not offer an opinion of our own on this subject well knowing that the judgement of an interested party, would weigh but little wise and discerning men" (7). The address goes on to show how low Hinckley rates of pay are in comparison with Nottingham even though the different nature of the work meant that there was no competition between them. The names of James Leigh, Thomas Brooks and Thomas Alsop appear at the foot of the document as spokesmen. Wages do not seem to have been raised as a result of this appeal. The following year a group of bakers, grocers and flour sellers met in a closed meeting to discuss organising to prevent the underselling of bread and flour. This combination of traders may have been a response to attacks on the supposedly outlawed truck system made in the Commission's report. A framework-knitter observer was excluded from the meeting but reported what he knew in a broadsheet addressed to the framework knitters and operatives of Hinckley. "The manufacturers of Leicester have agreed to give a small advance of wages, and it is to be hoped ours will follow so good a precedent, but what shall we be the better for it if this miserable clique can make us pay what price pleases them for our bread?" (8)The broadsheet calls on the operatives to "support with their hard earned money all such men" as sell goods in their shops for the market price. Again the name of James Leigh appears as a signatory to this document, together with Amos Foxon and Thomas Clews.

An undated document called for the formation of a organisation "uniting the whole Stocking Trade, comprehending the whole of our village population, for without their co-operation nothing effective can be done". The signatories recommended that "separate Unions be formed in each town and village with funds under the control of tradesmen, that they be held morally responsible for the carrying out of the legitimate objects of the society,- viz Protection to the Fair Tradesman - Upholding the Rights of Labour - and the Suppression of Truck" (9). This document was signed by representatives of both the wide and wrought branches of the trade with John Ginns,.as secretary for the wide branch and James Pratt for the wrought branch. A Hinckley man, Jabez Chaplin's name appears as overall chairman. A Jabez Chaplin achieved fame as the President of the Leicester Union. This person was born in 1860 into a family of many generations of framework knitters who at the age of 13 had tramped to Leicester in search of work. He joined the old Framework Knitters' Union in the late 1870's and, as a factory worker, he became one of the founder members of the Leicester Amalgamated Union in 1885 (10). The Jabez Chaplin who was chair of the Hinckley Union was probably the father of his more well-known namesake who carried on the trade union tradition. The fact that knitters were talking with the voice of trade unionists indicates an improvement in conditions of trade. In times of depression it was difficult to maintain any form of organisation especially in the framework knitting industry where workers were scattered in many small workshops and in domestic production and where subscriptions were difficult to collect, supposing they could be afforded at all. Relations between the workers and the employers did not improve and a leaflet from 1850 indicates that the knitters had resorted to strike action to try to obtain a regulation of prices in the wide frame branch of the industry. Unfortunately, any gains were usually temporary as organisation collapsed or deteriorated during the next slump.

The transition away from domestic production to workshop based manufacture helped in the move towards collectivity as it gathered a number of workers together but it was the coming of the factory that really made a difference to hosiery workers' living standards.

---

7 *The Address of the Hinckley Framework Knitters, to the public in general, Hinckley October 18, 1845, LRO DE1243/283*

8 *To the Framework Knitters and other Operatives of Hinckley, LRO DE 1243/284/2*

9 *To the Gentlemen, Tradesmen and the Public at large of Hinckley and its Vicinity, LRO DE1243/287*

10 *Richard Gurnham, 200 Years, The Hosiery Unions 1776-1976, Leicester, 1976 p66*

The Earl Shilton Strike and Libel Case, 1859

In the summer of 1859, two Earl Shilton hosiers, John Homer and Mr Everard, altered the system of payment agreed upon between employers and workers in the list of prices, by paying a uniform rate for all classes of work whether produced on wide or narrow frames. They were forced to do this, they claimed, because the extensive use of wide machinery in the production of wrought hose meant it was not profitable to use narrow frames making the wider and better types of goods that they were best suited for. Competition with other manufacturers was what caused them to make the reductions in wages. To compensate for the lowering of the rate for goods made on narrow frames, frame-rent would also be lowered from one shilling to sixpence a week. Unfortunately, wages fell from between 6d and 1s 6d. When notice of the change was given, the hands took work out as usual which they brought back the following Saturday. Some workers did not complain and took more yarn but others refused to do so (1). The next Monday an open air meeting was addressed by agitators, not Homer claimed, in the employ of himself or Mr Everard. Those assembled were told from the platform to tell their employers that unless the old system of payment was returned, narrow frames would be put out in the street.

Workmen employed by Mr Homer and Mr Everard, ceased work and refused to return until the statement prices were paid again in all branches of the trade. A letter from J Sketchley, the secretary of the Hinckley Committee, called for a levy of all workers in Hinckley and Earl Shilton of 6d a week for men and 3d weekly from women and boys (2). Amongst riotous yelling, workmen began to put out their frames. A group called the Hinckley Committee watched and encouraged the proceedings. They claimed that their employers had sent them to do it, threatening to reduce all prices for work by eightpence a dozen if it wasn't done. The other manufacturers were opposed to the practices of Homer and Everard as it threatened the system of frame rents. "To charge a shilling a week for a frame the average value of which does not exceed £3 10s and which at the present rate of smithying can be kept in repair for about fourpence a week is not a legitimate way of making a profit", claimed Homer in the Hinckley Journal (3). The strike lasted 15 weeks.

In another letter by Sketchley to the Midland Express, Homer was called a "truck-master". The owner of the newspaper, William Taunton, was sued for libel by the employer because he had allowed the letter to be published. Homer was asking for £10,000 in damages. The case attracted great interest and was reported on nationally. In the Times it was revealed that the framework knitters were paid a miserably low wage from which deductions were made for frame-rent, candles and other items. A frame cost £3 but about £2 10s rent per year was paid for it. Homer's wife owned a grocery store adjoining her husband's factory and about 200 of the 300 employees traded there. In the factory itself, no men were employed only women and girls. Taunton published no apology for the accusation in his newspaper and Homer did not exercise a right of reply. Homer submitted to the court that his wife had owned the shop before their marriage and that his employees chose to trade there. The court found in favour of Homer but awarded him only £5 damages.

Newspaper reports were sympathetic to the knitters. The Daily Telegraph stated that it would not argue with the verdict but pleaded the case of the framework-knitters. "We have no wish to impugn the justice of the verdict; and are willing to believe that the

1 *Hinckley Journal, 17 August 1859*
2 *Hinckley Journal, 30 July 1859*
3 *Hinckley Journal, 17 August 1859*

master stocking weaver of Hinckley had been maligned; that he did not grind the faces of his work-people; and that he had neither art nor part in the atrocious "truck" system. It appears that it is his wife who kept a grocer's shop in the town near his factory; and the proprietor of the Midland Express should have exercised more caution 'ere he inserted a statement calling a respectable manufacturer a truck-master. We dare say his wife sells very good groceries and if her husband's operatives choose to deal with her, it is surely libelious (sic) to construe into a compulsory system of barter that which may be only intended as a delicate complement to the good lady of the firm". "Facts, however, particularly when they are delivered on oath, are stubborn things; and although the plaintiff in this action is doubtless the kindest of masters and the most honourable of men, there seems to be no reason for disbelieving the evidence of two framework knitters examined, who swore that the earnings of "narrow frame workers", generally speaking, averaged from six to seven shillings a week. Moreover, it appears that this most miserable wage, this beggar's stipend, this pauper's fee, is subject to various deductions…" (4). Although not strictly breaking the Truck Act, the plaintiff was not working within the spirit of it.

Less sympathy was shown by the Leicestershire press, the Hinckley Journal printing only points favourable to the employer in its reports on the trial (5). Taunton did have some public sympathy though, a subscription list signed by 270 people each of whom donated a small sum in defence of the suit, attested by a clergyman as residents in the parish, was reported upon in an article in the London Times (6). However the Hinckley Journal dismissed the same list by saying that the judge had mentioned it in his summation "but that he thought very little of the clergyman who signed it". Despite the small award to Homer, Taunton was left facing legal and other expenses of £650, an immense debt in those days. Taunton was forced to sell his interest in the newspaper but was offered a job in London. He later achieved some fame as an actor under the name of Walter Pelham (7).

"I am a man, and whatever interests man interests me."
Terence.

TO THE

PUBLIC OF HINCKLEY

AND DISTRICT, AND THE

TRADE GENERALLY

OF THE THREE COUNTIES.

GENTLEMEN,—We beg most respectfully to call your attention to the unfortunate struggle now going on at Earl Shilton, between Messrs. Homer and Everard, Manufacturers, and those of their workmen who were engaged in the narrow-wrought hose branch. From the early part of March last, Mr. Evarard refused to pay the same rate of wages on certain sorts of goods as were paid by the other manufacturers of the district, the result was that after that Gentleman had been solicited several times to pay the proper rate of wages and he still refusing, those of his workmen who were engaged on the particular sorts in question ceased from labour, when the struggle had continued several weeks, Mr. Homer came forward and joining Mr Everard, laid a proposal before their workmen which materially altered the nature of the struggle. Three weeks ago those Gentlemen proposed to reduce the rent of their narrow frames from 1s to 6d per week, but at the same time proposed such a reduction in the wages of their workmen as would amount to from 6d. to 1s. 6d per week.

When we consider the fact that if those Gentlemen succeed in forcing their workmen to accept the above reduction, the whole of the Manufacturers of the district must of necessity follow the same course, it will be seen that it is a question of great importance, not only to the workman of this district but to the framework-knitters in the whole of the three counties. Let not the public suppose for a moment that the above reduction would be confined to the narrow wrought hose branch, the experience of the past tells us that that reduction would soon become general in every branch of the trade.

If we suppose the number of frames in the district amount to 2000, and that the proposed reduction would amount to but 6d per week each, it would take from the small earnings of the workmen the enormous sum of £50 per week, and would, therefore, most seriously affect the interests of the whole district. And when we add that we are assured by the majority of the Manufacturers of Hinckley that there is no need for any reduction, it will be admitted that in resisting it the men are but doing their duty to themselves, their families and the trade generally, and are struggling to uphold the interests of the whole district.

As in struggles of this kind those engaged therein must suffer great privations, and as those privations must be felt by the children as well as their parents, we hope and trust we shall not appeal in vain to your sympathies on their behalf. The number on strike is about 130.

In conclusion we beg to state that the workmen of Hinckley and the Villages, with one exception, have done their duty nobly, and we beg most respectfully to thank those of the Clergy, Gentry, and Tradesmen who have so generously tendered their support to the workmen during the last fortnight, and we hope for a continuance of the same. To the working men of Leicester who have so nobly come forward to our assistance we return our sincere thanks, and hope for a continuance of their support.

Signed on behalf of the Committee,

JOHN GINNS, Chairman.
J. SKETCHLEY, Secretary.

Hinckley, May 30, 1859

J. SIDDONS, Printer, Pocklington's Walk, Leicester.

4 *Daily Telegraph, 22 December 1859*
5 *Hinckley Journal, 23 December 1859*
6 *London Times, 22 December 1859*
7 *Betsy G Miller, William Frederic Taunton Sued for Libel, undated document in LRO P155/5/1*

Hinckley Hungers Yet Again - The Cotton Famine

Hinckley is not isolated from world events and in the 1860's a bitter conflict on the other side of the Atlantic brought hunger and despair to the hosiery workers of the community. Hinckley's staple product was wrought cotton hose, the raw material for which was supplied by the labour of slaves in the southern states of America. The American Civil War not only disrupted cotton production but the blockade by the Northern Federal navy of Southern ports prevented almost all of what cotton was available from being exported, despite the activities of some blockade runners. The Lancashire cotton industry was hit terribly by the "cotton famine" as it became known which lasted from 1862 to 1865. Factories closed down and workers were forced to claim relief under the Poor Law. The local parishes could not cope with the sheer quantity of people claiming assistance and relief committees were set up to appeal for aid nationally and to distribute donations to the needy. Lancashire cotton workers were forced to pawn their possessions, some were reduced to begging, others worked on labour schemes which often involved heavy manual work which they were not used to. Lancashire was the focus of public concern and charitable efforts to relieve those affected so severely by the cotton famine. Hinckley was affected just as harshly if not more so. At least Lancashire cotton workers had had some prosperity of sorts before the catastrophe and therefore had possessions to pawn. Not that this was anything but a marginal advantage as the famine lasted for three years. But Hinckley people had had no such prosperous times and were immediately plunged into the bitterest poverty. Thousands were totally out of work and had to be relieved by the parish and charitable efforts.

The crisis began in January 1862, when a Hinckley Journal article on the state of trade reported that the hosiery trade in the town was in a moderately healthy state with all hands pretty well employed. The demand for goods was not so much in excess as on some previous occasions at that season of the year. "Much anxiety is felt regarding the American affair" was an innocuous remark ominously closing the report (1). A week later the same paper reported that "the hosiery trade has not been so buoyant this week as for several weeks past in consequence of the difficulty of obtaining cotton" (2). On 25 January it was reported that "in the hosiery branch great difficulty is felt in obtaining cotton, the scarcity and advanced price of which militates very materially against both manufacturers and operatives; consequently a much less quantity of work has been given out. Some of the circular hose factories are also working short-time. The unsettled state of America is attributed to the cause"(3).

By March there was considerable falling off in the hosiery trade and work was becoming scarce. Many hands were quite out of employ. This was at the time of year when there was usually most demand. Future prospects showed no way of changing . May showed that the cotton famine was affecting not just those working with the material but other sections too. In Leicester and other places in the county where wool and worsted was normally worked, operatives were only partially employed as trade was "greatly affected by the distress of the cotton districts, where the demand is usually most extensive" (5). The inability of the industrial workers of Lancashire, usually relatively affluent with good combined family wages, to function as consumers was now hitting other areas. In Hinckley the hosiery trade was even more heavily depressed, news from America had put up the price of cotton even higher, and a large number of operatives were out of employ. On 10 May it was reported that "the depression in the hosiery trade is very heavy, sad but little work

1 *Hinckley Journal, January 11, 1862*
2 *Hinckley Journal, January 18, 1862*
3 *Hinckley Journal, January 25, 1862*
4 *Hinckley Journal, March 15 and 22, 1862*
Hinckley Journal, May 3, 1862

AN ACCOUNT OF THE MONIES RECEIVED AND EXPENDED

BY THE

Hinckley District Relief Committee.

Subscriptions Received.

	£	s.	d.
From Barwell, inclusive of £60 from Oakley Hall, ..	136	2	0
From Burbage, inclusive of Lady Cowper's and others,	149	11	0
Earl's Shilton,	162	1	4
Hinckley,	453	11	6
Leicester,	615	15	7
Society of Friends,	400	0	0
Mansion House,	1000	0	0
Central Committee at Manchester,	1100	0	0
General Sources,	2063	2	5
	£6080	3	10

Grants of Relief and other Expenditure.

	£	s.	d.
To Barwell,	712	8	11
Burbage,	644	3	11
Earl's Shilton,	992	10	4
Hinckley, inclusive of Relieving Officer's Salary, ...	3326	5	2
Advertisements,	80	1	6
Printing and Stationery,	33	1	3
Labour upon Public Works at Hinckley, inclusive of certain necessary material and implements, ..	121	15	9
Ditto at Sewing Schools,	27	0	0
Blankets,	100	0	0
In Bank,	42	17	0
	£6080	3	10

☞ 195 Barrels of Flour, 50 Sides of Bacon, 100 Tons of Coal, and Left-off Wearing Apparel, in addition to the above, were received and divided according to population.

(*Signed*)

W. SKIRROW, *Chairman.*

W. G. FARMER, } *Hon. Secs.*
JOHN ATKINS, }

JULY, 1864.

[illegible], PRINTER, HINCKLEY

has been given out from the warehouses this week. A great amount of distress prevails amongst the labouring classes" (6). The distress amongst the labouring classes did not result in any major changes to the numbers claiming relief. In the Board of Guardians' Report on 15 May they counted only 153 in the Workhouse a rise of only 5 on the same time the year before. The number of outdoor poor had risen to 1,300 from 1,134 the previous year, rise of only 166 claimants. Total expenditure on relief by the parish had increased to £80 9s 9 1/2d from £77 15s 10d the year before . This may show reluctance to claim relief rather than lack of need, the Poor Law regulations were very stringent and many people were too proud to allow themselves to be classed as paupers.

The Hinckley Journal tried to be optimistic reporting in July that trade was improving a little, some firms were giving out work but others were still only giving out as little as possible (8). The warehousemen and factory operatives at Atkins Brothers hosiery manufacturers still had their annual entertainment, held at the Baths. "They were provided with plenty of tea and other necessary consumables to which they did ample justice; after which cricket and quoits and other games were played by the male portion of the work people". "Women and girls enjoyed themselves in their usual games" (9) but what those games were is not mentioned in the report. If the workers were not in full employment then the meal would have been extremely welcome. No wonder they did it ample justice.

Although full employment was expected in Leicester in August, the Hinckley trade continued in a miserably distressed state. The manufacturers could not work with the high cost of cotton. "A great amount of suffering exists among the workpeople, many of whom have left the town and gone to Leicester and other districts in search of employment" (10). By September the manufacturers were expecting to have to close down their establishments altogether. There was no improvement by November when the depression in the cotton hosiery trade was still on the increase, very little work was given out. "Many families were quite destitute and the prospects for the coming winter were gloomy and discouraging". All classes were now feeling the effects of bad trade (11). Things were so bad a relief fund was established to help the starving workers. The manufacturers William Sills, T Goadby and Atkins Brothers donated £50 each, George Woodcock gave £30, Moore and Morley £26 5 shillings, Thomas Payne, Thomas Abell and Thomas Flavell each contributed £25. Lord Howe gave £100.

Efforts to assist the Hinckley hosiery workers were not confined to the charity of the middle class. On 20 December a working-men's meeting was held in solidarity by Leicester workers. Two men, former chartists of the 1840's and long time working class activists, Parker and Warner spoke in solidarity with their fellow workers in Hinckley. They called for all Leicester workers to contribute a penny a week subscription to go to help their needy fellow workers of Hinckley and all agreed that the rich should pay more (12).

The suffering people of Hinckley needed the assistance of their sympathisers for many months. Committees of gentlemen were formed, who in addition to their ordinary meetings, met fortnightly to hear the cases, and distribute the money and clothing that had been received. The manufacturers themselves donated and solicited help through their business connections. Businesses who had any market for their goods in Hinckley contributed and collections were made in places of worship and in the households of distinguished local gentlemen. The Moira and Swadlincote Colliery Companies gave 150 tons of coal, the Duke of Rutland subscribed £50 and Earl Howe £100. The Mansion House Committee, which was sending relief up to Lancashire also sent several large sums. A large donation was received from the Manchester relief fund. Altogether the amount received in money was about £8,000 besides gifts of blankets and clothing. The ladies of the town held meetings, established sewing schools, opened soup kitchens and helped the poor however they could. Road improvements provided partial employment for some of the men to keep them occupied and to make the funds last as long as possible. The Hinckley relief organisations were similar to the committees and activities that were established in Lancashire to help victims of the cotton famine there (13).

Things did not get back to normal until peace returned in the re-united States of America. The supply of cotton was restored produced now by free labour and not by slaves.

6 *Hinckley Journal, May 10, 1862*
7 *Hinckley Journal, May 17, 1862*
8 *Hinckley Journal, July 12 and 26, 1862*
9 *Hinckley Journal, July 19, 1862*
10 *Hinckley Journal, August, 23, 1862*
11 *Hinckley Journal, November 8, 1862*
12 *Hinckley Journal, December 20, 1862*
13 *Norman Longmate, The Hungry Mills, London, 1978*

Fireside to Frameshop to Factory

'Swift' winder - Wigston Framework Knitters Museum

In the early days of its development the industry was domestic or cottage based, the knitting frames would have been situated in the knitters' houses. In a modest house this would have been in the downstairs living area. In a small house with just one room upstairs and one down this must have been very crowded. The frame itself took up a lot of space and needed to be situated where it was warm and with the maximum light possible, a problem on the ground floor of houses built closely together and overshadowing each other. The stockinger and the rest of the household would have worked and lived in the same space, although in the warmer months the door could be left open and some tasks like seaming performed outside. To allow as much natural light as possible into the work area, some houses had long windows added. This was not an ideal way to work and those who found it possible used a separate room for their frames, sometimes building one on the back of their house or even having a workshop built in the backyard. Middlemen or hosiers might also have paid for the adaptations to existing houses which they then rented out to knitters.

Having a separate workshop or frameshop would allow the knitter to have more frames to enable the household income to be augmented by having more family members working or by taking on apprentices or even working with other journeyman knitters. Although the framework knitters worked singularly or in small units, they were often part of a large workforce employed by the same hosier. For instance in 1844, Joshua Clarke employed about 300 frames in Hinckley and 4 or 5 neighbouring villages (1), all working on wrought cotton hose. George Woodcock employed about 400 frames working on wrought hosiery. William Sills was a major employer with about 800 frames. The frameshop was often referred to as a factory by contemporaries, although unlike a modern factory it had no artificial power. As frames were usually rented from a hosier or middleman this would not have involved the knitter himself in any capital outlay, but more frame-rent would have to be paid. This would not be a problem while there was plenty of work but if a large household were all dependent on knitting for an income and frame rent had to be paid whether working or not, this kind of expansion could have been a financial gamble. These frameshops again would have needed plenty of light so that the knitters could see to perform the sometimes intricate tasks associated with hand-frame knitting. Elongated windows were built into these workshops and artificial light for darker days and night time working was provided by candles. Candle-light could be intensified by standing the candle behind a water-filled glass ball which magnified its light. This ingenious idea not only intensified the light and so prolonged the amount of time that the knitter could work but saved money on buying candles as one could be used rather than a greater number. The cost of candles came out of the knitter's income so any saving was welcome.

In some parts of the East Midlands knitting frames were placed in topshops built over the knitters' houses. These would have a row of long windows on the top storey of the building to allow light to enter the working area. Because of the weight and size of the frame, the framesmith would probably have put the frame together actually in the topshop and the floor would have had to be reinforced. In Hinckley, a ground floor room of the stockinger's home or a separate frameshop were favoured, initially perhaps, after enclosure moved farmers out into the countryside, adaptations of old agricultural buildings. The use of a wide-frame also made a frameshop more practical than accommodation within the house itself, although even as late as 1844, there were only 30 of these in Hinckley compared with 1,700

1 *1st Appendix to the Report on the Condition of the Framework Knitters, 1845, p99*

2 *W Felkin, An Account of the Machine-wrought Hosiery Trade: its extent and the condition of the framework-knitters; a paper read in the statistical section, at the second York meeting of the British Association, held September 18th 1844, together with evidence given under the Hosiery Commission Inquiry, London and Nottingham, 1845*

Wide Knitting Frame in Frameshop. Wigston FWKS Museum

narrow frames making fashioned hose (2). Sills and Woodcock had just introduced a few wide frames (3). A wander around the back lanes and alleys of the town will reveal many examples of old frameshops, most of them readapted to modern uses. A fully equipped frameshop which is open to visitors, is preserved at the Framework Knitter's Museum at Wigston in Leicestershire.

Sometimes frameshops were built by hosiers and middlemen aiming to increase the efficiency of production by their knitters by gathering them under one roof where they could be supervised. The hosier did not lose his income from frame rents as he now charged the knitters rent for the space occupied by the frames they worked as well as for the frame itself. Oil, candles, coal and even frame maintenance costs were deducted from the knitter's gross income. For efficiency, production could be broken down into a series of tasks and work passed between the frames to save time altering the width and other settings for different parts of a garment. According to the evidence of Thomas Smith to the Commission of Inquiry " a shop of 8 frames was considered large in his younger days but in recent years shops to house 40 or 50 frames have been built"(5). He made his statement in 1844. Large frameshops were unusual in Hinckley. Edward Kem Jarvis had experimented with a large factory at which, unusually, neither frame rent nor standing charge was made. His project failed because of the opposition of the framework knitters themselves to the regular routine which factory discipline imposed upon them(6).

Hosiery work was often seasonal, concentrating on production for the high demand of the colder months. The Hinckley season began at the end of November and lasted until the beginning of May. For the rest of the year trade in wrought brown cotton hose, the staple of the town, was very flat (7). At other times and in the frequent times of depression in the trade work was less plentiful. Even in a week of full employment days were lost, usually on Saturday, when the work was collected or taken to the hosier and payment received. Often the knitters were kept waiting for a new supply of yarn to make up or just decided to spend their pay and enjoy themselves for a few days which would mean no work was done on Monday and not much on Tuesday either. Knitters would then be forced to work exceptionally long hours, sometimes into the night on Thursday and Friday to complete their work on time for the Saturday collection. The Cadeby knitters collected materials on Sunday but no money. For their wages they went to Hinckley on Monday morning, where the hosier kept a grocery shop (8). This irregular pattern of working was what often inspired the hosier to gather his workers together in the frameshop in an attempt to impose discipline on their working habits.

Information about the quantity, value, ownership and proprietorship of properties used in Hinckley for purposes connected with the hosiery trade can be gleaned from records collected for rate assessments. The valuation of the houses and appurtenances of Hinckley dated January 1782 shows names associated with the industry as proprietors or occupiers of several houses indicating that they were renting them out to other members of the community (9). For instance, Thomas Hurst was both occupier and proprietor of a combshop. He was also proprietor and occupier of a house and proprietor of two other houses, occupied by Edward Ashby and Samuel Goode. Hurst's own home was worth only £1, the same value as those of his tenants. Thomas Atkins occupied a house and a warehouse from where

---

3 1st App to Rep on Condition of Framework Knitters, p 252-254, Victoria County Histories, History of Leicestershire, Vol III, p12
5 1st App to Report on Condition of Framework Knitters, p138
6 1st App to Report on the Condition of Framework Knitters, p210
7 1st Appendix to the Report on the Condition of Framework Knitters, pp 200, 205; Victoria County History, History of Leicestershire, Vol III, p12
8 Victoria County History, p7
9 Valuation of Houses and Apurtenances of Hinckley, 11 January 1782, LRO

he conducted his business worth together £3 10 shillings which were leased from Joseph Preston. A warehouse describes the place from which a hosier would give out and collect as well as store his yarns and finished products. Thomas Turner owned and occupied a house and warehouse worth £4.10d, whilst John Turner had a house and warehouse worth £10. William Bolesworth occupied a house and shop worth £1 15s, leased from a relative, probably his widowed mother, Sarah, herself living in a house of the same value. A "shop" does not necessary indicate retail premises, the name was used to describe a workshop also. The Bolesworth family has a long involvement in hosiery in the town and in the mid-eighteenth century John Bolesworth was taking on apprentices. William Hurst owned seven houses that were rented out. William Brown was occupier of a warehouse on Stockwell Head valued at £5 owned by Sarah Brown who lived in her own house worth £7. She also owned five other smaller houses ranging in value from 15 shillings to £1 15 shillings. The Illiff family owned a number of properties; John had one worth only 15 shillings and another occupied by James worth £1 15 shillings. Joseph leased a house and garden valued at £1 15 shillings from the Great Feoffment, owned and lived in another worth £9 10 shillings and rented out two small ones to Charles Challoner and Samuel Wickes. Sadly, this document does not record how many domestic premises housed knittting frames.

Winding Machine- Wigston Framework Knitters Museum

Poor Rate assessments also give an indication of the amount of property in industrial use. The first factory actually described as such as distinct from a workshop was that of William Williamson (10). The site of this building was on Upper Bond Street, fronting onto Factory Road, the former premises of Simpkin, Son and Emery Limited (11). Another source cites Joshua Clarke as the first person to attempt to introduce the factory system into the town (12). He fitted up extensive premises, the former wool-comber William Brown's workshop, in Stockwell Head with a great number of wide frames. These and the other early "factories" were not powered, they still housed manually operated machinery. Factory here is used in the sense of a place where things were made.

The Church Rate list gives descriptions of property, proprietors and occupiers. In 1844 two buildings described as factories are listed (13). John Marvin leased premises containing a house and factory together worth £14 13s 6d. A firm called Marvin Brothers was still in business in Earl Shilton during the post Second World War period. Someone called Marshall Marvin of Earl Shilton was taking on apprentices in 1802. The other factory was Jarvis Berford and Company, a much larger enterprise occupying buildings valued at £52 13s 6d. Both these factories included a house on site. Eleven warehouses are also listed, including that of Boultbee Brooks, a framesmith. The remaining ten were occupied by people from families known from other sources to have been in the hosiery business: Nicholas Ward, William Lee, Thomas Reddalls, John Glover of Wood Street, John Adkins, George Woodcock, David Gillespie, Thomas Murcott, William

10 *A J Pickering, The Cradle and Home of the Hosiery Trade, Hinckley, 1945, p48. On page 51 Pickering gives the factory proprietor's name as Wilkinson, which seems to be a misprint. listed in the Parish Rate Book of 1836.*
11 *A J Pickering, Cradle and Home of the Hosiery Trade, Hinckley, 1945, p51*
12 *Hinckley Parish Magazine, April 1874, p11*
13 *Church Rate Book, Hinckley 1844, LRO*

Henry Law and Henry Miles Ward. Dye shops were also being used by William Henry Law. William Cowdell rented property from Mary Sansome which included spinning rooms. Three young boys with the name Cowdell came to Hinckley as pauper apprentices in 1747, 1791 and 1798 from the Leire area. Perhaps William was a son or grandson of one of them. Many other premises were listed as houses with shops. Although some would be retail premises many could have been frameshops occupied by knitters working with yarn from the warehouses listed or from middlemen or bagmen from Leicester.

Mechanical power was not applied in the knitting industry until relatively late, compared with other branches of the textile industry, such as wool and cotton spinning and weaving. These were at the leading edge of industrialisation, having made use of water powered mills in the eighteenth century before pioneering steam driven factory machinery. Technological improvements needed to be made to the knitting frame before power could be applied to it. Experiments with circular machines had been conducted by Marc Isambard Brunel who patented a steam-powered circular machine in 1816. This was not taken-up in the trade however and no more applications of circular motion were taken up until the late 1830's. Steam power was rotary power and circular motion that could be continuous was much more suited to adaptation to steam power than the hand frame that was operated with a number of discontinuous, separate movements. Matthew Townshend's invention of the latch needle in 1847 also helped progress the move to apply power to knitting machinery. The first powered hosiery factory in Leicestershire was that of Cartwright and Warner in Loughborough which opened in about 1840 (14) .

The first steam powered factory to open in Hinckley was that of Thomas Payne. He had seen some of M'Clawson's (sic) machines exhibited at the Bulls Head. After seeing the machines working and finding the samples produced satisfactory, he decided to purchase some for himself.

The patentee and contractor agree to complete their respective work within two months or if in default, to pay £1 for every day beyond the agreed time

Victorian factory building on Factory Road, Hinckley, Daniel Payne and Son.

for completion of the 40 machines required (15). The factory opened in 1855 in premises between Castle Street and Wood Street to which the firm fronted. The site had been purchased by Payne from John Glover, another hosier, in 1848. In the Church Rate List of 1844, John Glover's property was described as a house and warehouse. Payne's Wood Street factory had an engine and boiler that powered 40 "heads" of circular machines. After sixteen years the factory was bought by William Crow in 1871 when Thomas Payne retired to the seaside at Dawlish (16). Crow went into partnership with William Truslove but in 1892, after going into receivership, the premises were taken over by Joseph Ginns and Arthur Davenport who were joined by Joseph Moore in 1894 when the original partnership was dissolved. Arthur Davenport's own firm, a partnership with his sons was established in 1888, and in 1894 he dissolved not just his partnership with Joseph Moore but another short-lived one which had been Davenport and Miles. Ginns and Moore agreed a partnership in 1898 and the firm later became Ginns, Son and Moore that endured until recent years.

When Thomas Payne opened his factory workmen complained, fearing that this would ruin them, and manufacturers also thought it would

14 *Victoria County History of Leicestershire, Vol III, p16*
15 *Hinckley Parish Magazine, April 1874, p11*
16 *Pickering, p 51*

be injurious to business (16). There was no need for alarm. In a few years other manufacturers invested in powered factories themselves, creating new jobs without threatening the position of the existing framework knitters for about another twenty years.

Earl Shilton's first powered factory was established in about 1860 by James Toon. This was the first factory in Leicestershire outside the towns of Hinckley, Loughborough and Leicester (17).

A single water-filled boiler heated by a coal fire provided all the power for a factory. Steam produced by the boiler provided energy that could be converted into movement by an engine turning a fly-wheel. This rotary motion could provide power for all the machines on the site by having a belt attached to its wheel that in turn was attached to a smaller wheel moving more quickly which turned an axle or shaft. A series of other drive-belts would be connected to and turned by this shaft. Other shaft and drive-belts could be added to spread the power around the factory. Each machine was connected by this system of drive-belts to the steam engine which converted the source of power from steam produced by water and heat to rotary motion. All the machines started and finished at the same time as they were all driven by a single engine. If for some reason the drive-belt came off, then all the machines in the section had to stop. This imposed a social change as great as any in the industrial revolution. People had to start work at times set by the employer and have breaks when told and finish at a fixed time. Hours were fixed between 6 am and 6 pm in summer and 7 am and 7 pm in winter (18). They also had to go to work six days a week. If they failed to do so or were late they were punished by having wages stopped. They could not make up the time later. This also governed what time was available for socialising and family life.

Steam power at first could only be applied to circular knitting which produced a long tube of fabric which had to be cut up to make garments. For this reason it did not adversely affect the manual framework knitting industry for many years. The two branches of the industry, powered and manual, continued side by side until the late nineteenth century. Higher quality, fully-fashioned articles still had to be made using a hand frame. After experiments with narrowing the fabric in 1857 made by Arthur Paget of Loughborough and Luke Barton of Nottingham, William Cotton of Loughborough worked on widening fabric and in 1864 patented a fine gauge machine which could automatically widen and narrow. Soon, this machine was in wide use and Cotton set up a factory of his own producing a hundred machines a year by 1870 (19).

Even though powered production of hosiery was possible from the 1840's it was slow to develop, in Hinckley in particular. At the cheaper end of the market, circular powered machines were not much quicker at producing material for "cut-ups" than a hand frame which was now built wider to produce more at once, thereby competing very well with powered machinery (20). The market for manufactured goods generally increased with improved living standards and an increase in export markets due to improved communications. Along with it the demand for the product of the framework knitter also grew. The first decades of factory production, apart from during the American Civil War, were amongst the most prosperous ever for framework knitters. Many of them found additional work adding feet and finishing articles made on power frames (21). Wider frames were made, the carriers improved and larger workshops built housing more frames, each specialising in a particular part of the garment.

16 *Hinckley Parish Magazine, April 1874, p11*
17 *Richard Gurnham, 200 Years - The Hosiery Industry 1776-1976, Leicester, 1976, p51*
18 *Atkins of Hinckley, 1722-1995, privately published, undated paper*
19 *Marilyn Palmer, Framework Knitting, Shire Album 119, 1984, p27*
20 *Gurnham, p24*
21 *Gurnham, p25*

James Bennett Ltd, Steam Engine

Hosiers and middlemen were reluctant to abandon the existing system of domestic and workshop based production because of the frame rents it provided them with. Frame rents were finally abolished by statute in 1874. The irregularities of the framework knitting industry had produced workers who were not used to the discipline of regular working-hours and who valued their independence. It was therefore difficult for them to adapt to the idea of working in a factory with set starting and finishing and break times. There was also a ready supply of cheap labour, the knitter could make use of his wife and the children could be set to work winding, twisting and seaming. The Factory Acts' provisions that covered the new powered establishments forbade the employment of children under ten but workshop and domestic employment was exempt. This source of child labour was jeopardised by the Education Act of 1870 and destroyed completely in 1876 when compulsory education for children between the ages of 5 and 14 was introduced. The 1870s were therefore a turning point in the story of hosiery when the industry turned away from manual framework knitting towards powered factory work. However it wasn't until the 1890s that framework knitting began to disappear and some hand frames continued to be worked into the twentieth century. In some factories there were separate rooms housing hand frames which had been removed from the homes of knitters, thus bringing some framework knitters into the factory environment.

Even with the decline of framework knitting, the cottage or domestic side of the hosiery industry persisted with the adoption of the hand operated, circular Griswold knitting machines and the flat Lamb machines. These machines could change from rib to plain knit by simple adjustments, the Lambs could even do shaping. These machines were developed in America and British manufacturers took out patents to produce them in Britain. Griswold himself came to live and work in England. After being in partnership as Griswold and Hainsworth Ltd, Hosiery Manufacturers and patenting several innovations in knitting machine technology and a stocking specially adapted to the needs of cyclists. In 1881 he formed the London and Leicester Hosiery Company Ltd based on Winifred Street in Leicester. Other local firms were soon adapting and improving on the original Griswold machines. By 1898 the Leicester Co-operative Hosiery Manufacturing Society noted that the Griswold stocking knitters were "taking work back to the villages" which had been lost over past decades as urban factories replaced traditional village frameshops. Typical of this continuance and development of the domestic side of the industry alongside the factory system was Daniel Angrave. He was born into a family of framework knitters living in Gilmorton near Lutterworth. In 1895 he installed six Griswold knitters in a brick workshop built behind his cottage. His machines were purchased and serviced by I L Berridge & Co. of Leicester who had recently acquired Griswold's patent rights. The small circular knitters were clamped to worktables beneath windows along both sides of the upper storey of Angrave's workshop. This "topshop" was reached by a ladder near the entrance in the room below where children prepared yarn on a bobbin winder along the rear wall. Angrave travelled to Hinckley by pony and cart each Friday to his hosier's warehouse to collect yarn that was stored in a room over his cart house next to the workshop. In Hinckley he deposited the week's finished goods, usually around 800 pairs of socks, not counting those made by local women he supplied with yarn, who owned their own knitters. Each of the female workers normally made two dozen worsted socks a day, working from 8 O'clock in the morning until half past six in the evening with half hour breaks for dinner and tea. The toes were

The Knitters' Circular and Monthly Record.

An organ for the Hosiery Trade.

Telegraphic Address—"KNITTER, LEICESTER."

LEICESTER, JANUARY, 1894. [VOL. I.

ADDRESS FOR TELEGRAMS: "WILDT," LEICESTER.
NATIONAL TELEPHONE, No. 51.

H. WILDT & CO.,
LEICESTER,
Are now exhibiting at their premises
TERROT'S FRENCH
CIRCULAR FRAME
Boas-King
Automatic Knitter.
RESERVE PARTS, NEEDLES, &c.
ALWAYS KEPT IN STOCK.
REPAIRS on the premises at Leicester.
Price Lists, full Descriptions, Estimates for Single Frames or whole Plants by return of post.
MACHINES for the GLOVE TRADE

The "HARRISON" Patent Knitter

Works by hand, but can be fitted to work by power.

Made in sizes from 4 inches to 40 inches wide, and from 8 to 14 needles per inch.

THE "HARRISON" is the most perfect Knitting Machine for speed, perfect stitch, uniformity of fabric; in evenness and weight, finish, and the most durable; for which GOLD MEDALS and other Honours have been awarded at Paris, London, Barcelona, and elsewhere.

The HARRISON "SUN"
is a recently improved Circular Ribbed Knitting Machine, which knits most superior Ribbed Hose.

One customer, comparing it with other popular Machines, says, "It has many advantages which others do not possess."

Another customer says, "When I took my samples to a warehouse, they were so pleased at the superiority of the Ribbed Hose, that preferential orders were forthwith given to me, which have been continued & increased."

MANUFACTURED BY
WM. HARRISON,
48, UPPER BROOK STREET,
MANCHESTER.

Brushing showing drive belts, 1929, Manchester Hoiery

Circular Knnitting machine showing drive belts. James Bennett Ltd

closed by local female outworkers at 3d for a dozen pairs. When Angrave died his wife continued the business until after the First World War, with a local carrier taking the goods produced to Hinckley each week (22).

When Hinckley Technical College, now part of North Warwickshire and Hinckley College, was set up in 1891 under the Technical Instruction Act of 1889 framework knitting was one of the subjects offered at its outset and it continued to be taught into the 1900's (23). Among the first college governors was Mr John Atkins. The first classes of January 1892 included subjects relevant to the "trades of the town," hosiery, shoe-making, horticulture, "hand and eye" classes for grammar school boys and continuation classes. In August 1892, governors decided that framework knitting should be taught. In September of that year it was decided to increase the size of the framework knitting class. A suggested class size of 60 pupils was proposed but it was prudently thought that without consulting the teacher, 40 or 50 would be enough! The next month the new college hired a frame from Thomas Hanson for one pound. That framework knitters were still not affluent was indicated in 1894 by the governors writing to ask the County Council whether the 2 shilling fee for tuition should be charged to the framework knitting students, as it was for those of other trades. Arthur Davenport was part of a committee supervising frames being placed in the Grammar School, at that time the College had no premises of its own and hired rooms in schools and church halls around the town. By February 1895 the question was being asked, would it be better to hold the framework knitting class in factories? Arrangements were to be made with Davis and Son for the classes to be held there where the pupils could see the machines in motion. So important was the hosiery industry to the community, the technical college had a Hosiery Committee to advise it. Amongst its first members in 1895 were several familiar names from the industry and local community: Rev Davies, Mr Johnson, Mr Chapman, Mr Payne, Mr Chawner, J Smith, J Bolesworth, Arthur Davenport, J Biggs, Frank Goode with William Pickering as chairman. This relationship between the knitted textile trade and Hinckley College continues up to the present day. Hosiery factories needed better educated workers with technical skills to operate the ever more complex machinery. It was no longer practical or legally possible for children to learn the trade by gradual absorption and imitation of their parents or masters as they worked along side them from an early age. Training now had to be provided by the employers with the help of the "tech". Another change brought about through the development of the factory system.

Women became wage labourers in their own right, with individual incomes not part of a family wage. As knitting production increased so too did the demand for women auxiliary workers. In the earliest factories, women had worked as winders alongside men right from the start. Seaming was still done in the domestic sphere with women working as outworkers. From the 1870's improvements in steam-powered sewing machines brought more and more women into the factories as seamers and linkers, although a few worked on the knitting machines against the opposition of male workers who feared this would depress wages and undermine the status of the male knitter. From the 1880s the hand-cranked circular Griswold machines which knitted plain and ribbed hose at the turn of a handle provided another source of employment for women. The Griswolds and similar circular hand operated machines did not need a power source to work them and were small enough to be clamped to a table top. They were therefore ideal for working in the home. Home or outworking represented a survival of the domestic system well into the factory age and, though often poorly paid, survives today, especially amongst women with young families. By the end of the nineteenth century the Leicester hosiery workers' union began to fear women operating manual Griswolds as an economic threat to factory workers (24). The female section of the workforce comprised growing numbers of both young girls and married women (25). In 1890 women made up 63% of the total hosiery industry workforce, 15,630 workers out of a total of 24,838. By 1895 the proportion of women had risen to 72%, 24,427 out of 34,198 workers altogether. In 1904, women comprised three-quarters of all hosiery workers, 27,219 out of 36,336. The numbers of women employed in the trade had almost doubled between

---

22 Richard Candee, Domestic Industry in the Factory Age: Anglo-American Development of the 'Family' Knitting Machine, Textile History, Volume 29, Number 1, Spring 1998, pp 62-63

23 Hinckley Technical College Minute Books, 1891 onwards

24 Richard Candee, Domestic Industry in the Factory Age, Textile History, Volume 29, Number 1, Spring 1998, p83

25 Gurnham, p34

Women & Girls 'linking', T Jenniings and Sons Ltd

1890 and 1907 when there were 30,362 of them out of a total number of 39,971 employees. The number of men in the trade had remained almost static over the same period at a figure fluctuating at around nine and a half thousand. Improvements to knitting machines meant faster production without any more knitters, which created more employment for women in the auxiliary trades. Becoming a mender was another way a woman could earn a living. Menders were paid more than the seamers and stitchers and in the earlier period of the factory production were employed in warehouses (26). In Hinckley women workers came in from the neighbouring villages and the nearby town of Nuneaton whose own textile industry, ribbon-weaving was in the terminal stage of its decline. Many other women became employed as "outworkers" ,

With the aid of steam-power the weekly output of stockings in Hinckley had risen to over 30,000 dozen pairs. By 1894 there were over twenty factories in the Hinckley area including Hall's at Stoke Golding (27). The townscape became characterised by tall hosiery factory chimneys, typical of a Victorian industrial scene.

Factory workers were able to secure greater control of wages and working conditions for themselves through their unions than the hand frame knitters had been able to. When manual framework knitters began to face serious competition from the factories in the late 1870's their small craft unions were unable to resist attacks on their members wage rates. However, in Hinckley, wage rates in factories were lower than in bigger towns and therefore undercut the workers in Leicester, just as the framework knitters had done in the earlier period. By the 1880s Hinckley was notorious as a "hotbed of low prices". The framework knitters' union to which many factory workers had belonged had completely collapsed and because of victimisation by the employers, the factory hands had been unable to form a new union for themselves. Hinckley wages were amongst the lowest in the East Midlands and women and boys were freely employed on the smaller and more automatic machinery (28). Leicester firms were moving their businesses to the county where wages were lower, a threat to workers in the larger town who had just secured through a fortnight's strike action, a uniform wage list throughout the borough of Leicester.

To stop this under-cutting and to give Hinckley workers a decent wage a delegation was sent to Hinckley in 1886 led by James Holmes, the secretary of the Leicester Amalgamated Hosiery Union, begun in 1884 by power-knitters who had left the Framework Knitters' Union. Hinckley hosiery workers had to organise. The male knitters of two of Hinckley's largest factories, about 120 of them, joined the union after a number of meetings. Sadly, the employers at the two factories involved threatened to dismiss anyone in the union. Despite promises of support, all but two, who were sacked, left the union and the Hinckley branch was dead (29). Low wages gave Hinckley employers a competitive advantage and so they were determined to stamp out any attempt to form a union. Wages were cut further; in 1888 they had been reduced by three-farthings a dozen for circular knitting and most of the workers were on half-time. By 1890 the knitters could only earn about 16 shillings to 18 shillings a week when working full-time. This was only about two-thirds of the average wage in Leicester.

Hinckley workers were eager to improve their condition and when another attempt to unionise them was made by the Leicester Union in December 1890, they responded

26 Gurnham, p47
27 Victoria County History, p 16
28 Gurnham, p50
29 Gurnham, p51

To Mr William Buckler
of London

Dear Sir

We, the Trimmers and Warehousemen employed at the Hosiery Factories in Hinckley desire to express to you our sincere thanks for the hearty sympathy you have shown with your old fellow-townsmen during the recent crisis in the Hosiery Trade. For a period of ten weeks we were thrown out of employment and a large amount of distress prevailed amongst us. You were good enough to appeal on our behalf to the City Warehouses and by your prompt energy and influence raised a considerable sum of money for our relief. We shall long remember your kindness and the activity you displayed as soon as the matter was brought to your notice

Signed for the Trimmers and Warehousemen
Rev. A. Calvert. M.A. Chairman
Rev. A. L. Smith. B.A. Vice-Chairman
John Bray (Trimmer). Treasurer
Edwin Bedford (Warehouseman) Secretary
Officers of the Relief Committee

Hinckley
June 30th 1891

Misc 434

enthusiastically. Four hundred joined in just a month and in January 1891 Holmes started to draw up wage lists for the new branch ready for negotiations with the Hinckley employers (30). The employers refused to meet the officials and threatened to close down their factories rather than pay the wages on the list, (31) which had severe consequences. Almost every factory in the town came to a standstill in a nine week long strike that involved nearly 1,800 men, women and young people. This heroic action involving many sacrifices and much suffering secured the signing of the wage list by the employers, giving the hosiery workers wage increases of between 20 and 40 per cent. Hinckley workers did not win their victory entirely alone; they relied on the solidarity of fellow workers. To secure this victory, hosiery workers' unions around the Midlands, which were united in a Federation, had had to pool their financial resources, a drain on the funds of them all. Sympathisers contributed to collections to help sustain the stikers and their families, especially the elderly and children. The Leicester Union also recruited the majority of Earl Shilton workers and, after a long struggle there, managed to introduce the Hinckley list (32). In 1897 the Hinckley branch left the Leicester Union to start one of its own.

The end of the nineteenth century marked the end of the appalling poverty that had haunted those in the knitting industry for generations. Thankfully, better times at last were now on the way for those "in the hosiery".

30 Gurnham, p53
31 Bill Partridge, The Great Strike, Hinckley Times, 26 May 1989
32 Gurnham, p54

The Hosiery Trade in Leicestershire
Early Price Lists - Bill Partridge

Price Lists, Wage Agreements, Arbitration and Conciliation in the Hosiery Trade Between 1778 and 1898

This was the period which saw the stocking being produced by the framework knitter and his family, first in his cottage, then with several frames housed in a frame shop situated behind the master hosier's house, then, with the coming of mechanisation, in factories.

The hosier, with his middlemen and bagmen, changed to something approaching the modern day hosiery manufacturer.

Negotiated Rates

Price lists and wage agreements were negotiated between an association of employers on the one hand and the workers in combination, or as we understand it, in a trade union. With each agreement came an improvement in industrial relations, a degree of fairness and some security for the workers, also a better level of competition amongst the employers in the costs of production. Allied to an agreement on negotiated rates came a procedure for arbitration on disputes, where a small number of accepted representatives from the two sides could settle disputes without recourse to damaging strike action.

Before looking in detail at examples of price lists, the prevailing situation can usually bee highlighted by a brief summary of events. Before power-driven machines were installed in factories the trade was run by merchants based in cities or larger towns "putting-out" yaarn to framework knitters in cities, towns and the surrounding villages. The articles produced ranged from luxury goods such as stockings and gloves knitted in pure silk, to the more useful goods made from wool, worsted and cotton.

It was unusual for the hosiers to deal directly with the framework knitters, the yarn and instructions what to knit were given out to middlemen or to "undertakers". These "bagmen" operated around the villages where they dominated the knitters by oppressive practices, especially when trade was bad.

1787 – The framework knitters of the "Three Counties", Derby, Leicester and Nottingham, meeting in Nottingham, negotiated a list of minimum wage rates with hosiers.

1812 – Gravenor Henson, a Nottingham stockinger who later was to achieve fame as a writer of technical works and also on the social aspects of the trade, formed the "Union Society of Framework Knitters". Two years later this union was making rapid progress throughout Leicestershire, London, Godalming, Tewkesbury and Northamptonshire. The union laid down its own rates and struck against any firm that did not pay the rate. When three members of the committee were prosecuted under the Combination Laws the union collapsed.

A Brief Period of Prosperity

It was not always poverty in the trade. The years 1800 to 1810 witnessed orders for hosiery too vast to be knitted. At that time hosiers had to pay an advance on the price to bribe knitters to work for them rather than for a competitor.

1858 – A "Shirt and Drawers Union" was started in Leicestershire and by 1872 it had 1,000 members in the town of Leicester and a further 1,000 in the surrounding villages. In the same year, 1858, a "Sock and Top Union" was formed which by 1870 had 800 members. Both unions had agreed price lists with the hosiers by 1874.

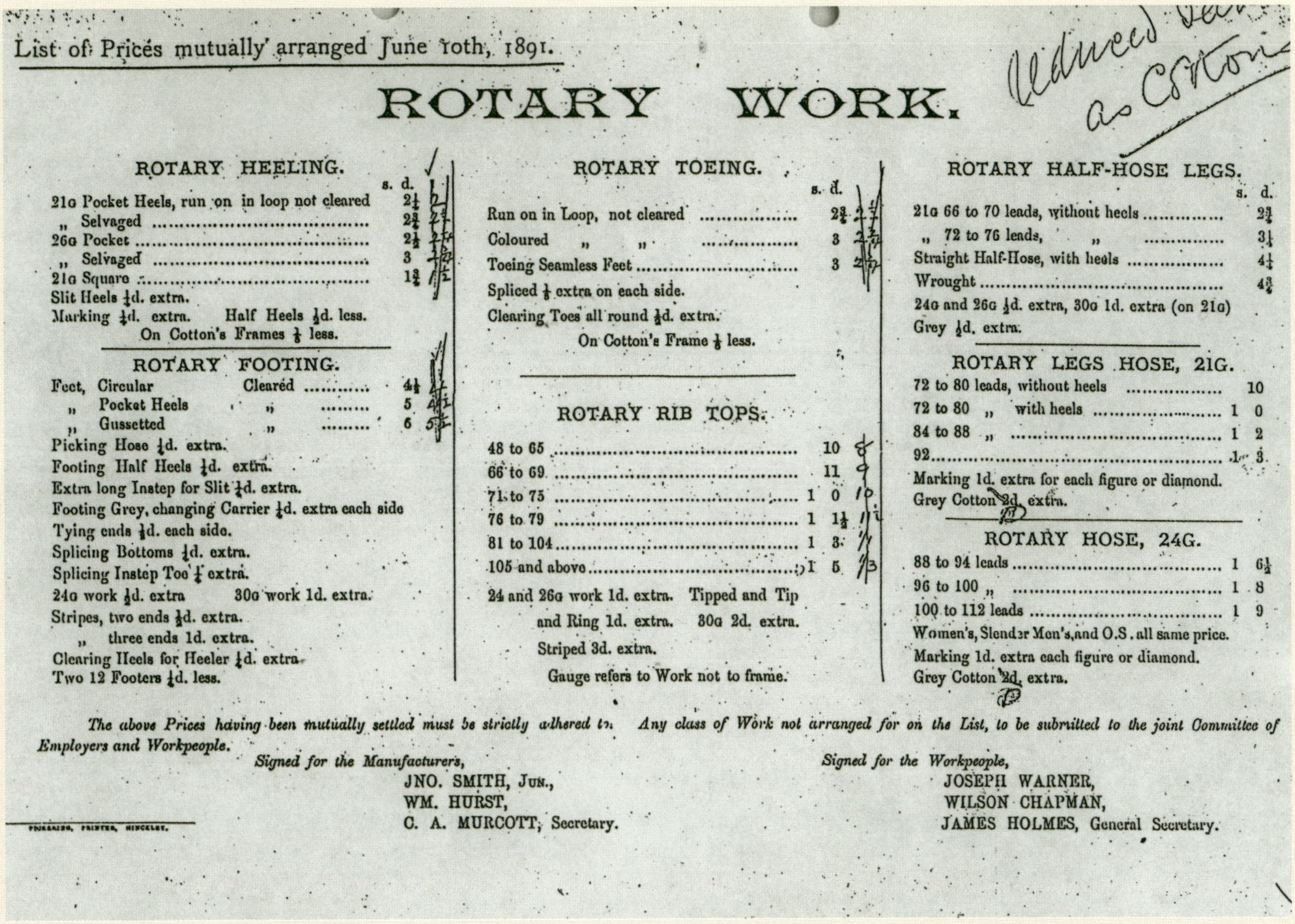

List of Prices mutually arranged June 10th, 1891.

ROTARY WORK.

ROTARY HEELING.

	s.	d.
21G Pocket Heels, run on in loop not cleared		2¼
„ Selvaged		2¾
26G Pocket		2½
„ Selvaged		3
21G Square		1¾

Slit Heels ¼d. extra.
Marking ¼d. extra. Half Heels ½d. less.
On Cotton's Frames ⅛ less.

ROTARY FOOTING.

		s.	d.
Feet, Circular	Cleared		4½
„ Pocket Heels	„		5
„ Gussetted	„		6

Picking Hose ¼d. extra.
Footing Half Heels ¼d. extra.
Extra long Instep for Slit ¼d. extra.
Footing Grey, changing Carrier ¼d. extra each side
Tying ends ½d. each side.
Splicing Bottoms ¼d. extra.
Splicing Instep Toe ¼ extra.
24G work ½d. extra 30G work 1d. extra.
Stripes, two ends ½d. extra.
„ three ends 1d. extra.
Clearing Heels for Heeler ¼d. extra
Two 12 Footers ¼d. less.

ROTARY TOEING.

	s.	d.
Run on in Loop, not cleared		2¾
Coloured „ „		3
Toeing Seamless Feet		3

Spliced ⅛ extra on each side.
Clearing Toes all round ½d. extra.
On Cotton's Frame ⅛ less.

ROTARY RIB TOPS.

	s.	d.
48 to 65		10
66 to 69		11
71 to 75	1	0
76 to 79	1	1½
81 to 104	1	3
105 and above	1	5

24 and 26G work 1d. extra. Tipped and Tip and Ring 1d. extra. 30G 2d. extra.
Striped 3d. extra.
Gauge refers to Work not to frame.

ROTARY HALF-HOSE LEGS.

	s.	d.
21G 66 to 70 leads, without heels		2¾
„ 72 to 76 leads, „		3¼
Straight Half-Hose, with heels		4¼
Wrought		4¾

24G and 26G ½d. extra, 30G 1d. extra (on 21G)
Grey ½d. extra.

ROTARY LEGS HOSE, 21G.

	s.	d.
72 to 80 leads, without heels		10
72 to 80 „ with heels	1	0
84 to 88 „	1	2
92	1	3

Marking 1d. extra for each figure or diamond.
Grey Cotton 2d. extra.

ROTARY HOSE, 24G.

	s.	d.
88 to 94 leads	1	6½
96 to 100 „	1	8
100 to 112 leads	1	9

Women's, Slender Men's, and O.S. all same price.
Marking 1d. extra each figure or diamond.
Grey Cotton 2d. extra.

The above Prices having been mutually settled must be strictly adhered to. Any class of Work not arranged for on the List, to be submitted to the joint Committee of Employers and Workpeople.

Signed for the Manufacturers,
JNO. SMITH, Jun.,
WM. HURST,
C. A. MURCOTT, Secretary.

Signed for the Workpeople,
JOSEPH WARNER,
WILSON CHAPMAN,
JAMES HOLMES, General Secretary.

Conciliation and Arbitration

A series of strikes in the various branches of framework knitting in Nottingham was very disruptive to the trade in general. In 1860 a Nottingham hosier, A J Mundella, brought peace by persuading the hosiers and the workpeople to agree to the creation of a Conciliation Board, something unique to British industry at that time. The Board, consisting of nine of the leading hosiers and nine representatives of the workpeople met every three months. The Board's "Committee of Inquiry" met as frequently as was necessary, at a week's notice.

1861 – The Nottingham hosiers agreed to ensure that their middlemen did not obtain a frame rent from their workers. In 1866 a similar undertaking was obtained from the Sutton and Mansfield hosiers.

1867 – Uniform piece rates had been established from every branch of the hand frame trade union Nottingham and the surrounding towns and villages.

1875 – Uniform price lists were effective in Leicester.

1892 – The number of hand frames still working in the Midlands was estimated at 5,000. From the earliest times the hand frame knitters had used an apprenticeship scheme for training new workers. With the demise of their craft the apprenticeship traditions had collapsed and the new breed of factory workers made no attempt to revive them.

Many small craft unions were started, such as the "Circular Framework Knitters' Society" in 1857 for workers operating the new "roundabouts" as circular machines were known. In 1865 the "United Rotary Power Framework Knitters' Society" for those operating the large flat or rotating machines. The "Seamers' and Stitchers' Union" was formed in 1874 and in 1875 the "Menders' Society". None of these small unions could pay out any benefits such as sick pay from their tiny subscriptions. In Leicester the "Framework Knitters' Union" was formed in 1884 by 500 machine knitters and 100 lamb machine knitters. The first secretary, paid full time, was James Holmes; we shall hear of him later in Hinckley in 1891.

The published price lists contain, as well as the prices for the different jobs, points of general interest and details of the machinery then in use, the styles of hosiery of the time and the yarns being knitted.

A statement agreed by the hosiers in Leicester on 27 May 1830, includes the phrase "Worsted and Lamb's Wool Dumps" which requires explanation. At that time many classes of stockings for both men and women were ornamented at the instep, the ankle and the calf with embroidered clocks

List of Prices mutually arranged June 10th, 1891.

KNIT LIST.

CIRCULAR HOSE.

		s.	d.
Plain or Self Toes, White Tops	per doz.		1½
Red Striped Welt and Tip, White Toes	„		2
Ribbed Hose	„		2

Loop Wheel or Bearded Needle ¼d. less.

		s.	d.
Hose, White Tops and Toes			1¾

CIRCULAR HALF-HOSE.

		s.	d.
Without Top	per score	1	3
Cleared Top Bundle	„	4	7
Round Feet Bag Heels, Self	„	3	9
„ „ „ White Toes	„	4	0
Narrow Toe Half-Hose Legs	„	3	4

ROTARY.

	s.	d.
Half-Hose Legs, 44 to 56 leads		4½
Hose Legs	1	0

Clearing Tops ½d. extra.

	s.	d.
Square Heels, Run on		1½
Fashioned Heels		2¼
Rotary Feet, Narrow Toe		4¼
Instep and Bottoms		4¾
Fashioned Gusset		5½
Instep Length of Heels		5
Bottoms Gussetted		3

Clearing Insteps ¼d. extra.

Clearing all round ½d. extra.

COTTON'S PATENT.

	s.	d.
Narrow Toe Feet		3¼
Instep and Bottoms		3¾
Fashioned Gusset		4½

Tied ends ½d. extra each side.

Changing carriers ¼d. extra each side.

PATENT KNIT HOSE.

		s.	d.
Legs, without Insteps, set on or Welted	per doz.		7½
Legs, with Insteps	„		9

PATENT KNIT HALF-HOSE.

		s.	d.
Without Insteps	per doz.		3½
With Insteps	„		5

Toes and Heels ¼d. less than Rotary.

KNITS.

		s.	d.
Linking Heels	per 100	5	0
„ Toes	„	5	0
Circular Heels and Toes	per doz.		1¼
Putting on Tops	„		1¾
Bag Feet and Heels	„		1½
Hose with Bits	per 100	6	0

STITCHING.

Same Price as Plain Hose.

CIRCULAR RIB TOPS.

	s.	d.
One-Feeder, Brown and White		6
„ „ Coloured and Grey		7

Welt and Slack Course 1d. extra.

Tipped 1½d. extra.

	s.	d.
Two-Feeder Frames, Brown or White		4½
„ „ Coloured		5½

If cut 1d. extra.

Welted Tops cut 2d. extra.

The above Prices having been mutually settled must be strictly adhered to. Any class of Work not arranged for on the List, to be submitted to the joint Committee of Employers and Workpeople.

Signed for the Manufacturers,
JNO. SMITH, Jun.,
WM. HURST,
C. A. MURCOTT, Secretary.

Signed for the Workpeople,
JOSEPH WARNER,
WILSON CHAPMAN,
JAMES HOLMES, General Secretary.

PICKERING, PRINTER, HINCKLEY.

(clox) of varying shape and style. It was then the common practice to refer to a stocking that did not have this decoration as a "Dump". "The Hands must subscribe three pence per week" could refer to the charge levied on knitters who were working in a frame shop. In 1830 Leicester was mainly engaged in knitting wool and worsted hose but as cotton was the prominent yarn used in Hinckley the document states that for "the Cotton Hose under 24 Gages (sic) to be guided by the Hinckley Statement".

On 8th April 1873 an important meeting was held in Hinckley. By careful reading of the Price List issued as a result of this meeting we can learn much of the trade of that time. On the one side of the negotiations were five hosiers who signed as Manufacturers. The other side signed as framework knitters who represented Hinckley, Barwell, Burbage and Earl Shilton. The prices were agreed upon "from the list dated January 23rd 1872", so there had been at least one earlier agreement on prices. The List contains the statement "Rent for single frames not more than 9d per week". This would apply to frames similar to the one dating from the 1740s which is in Hinckley Museum. It would also apply to any frames being worked in the Knitter's home although at that time most of the frames had been brought into frame shops. The list also agrees to variations on the prices "in case frame rents be abolished". This was because in 1873 a Bill to forbid the charging of frame rents was before Parliament. The Act was passed in 1874. "The above prices will be paid on all work taken in on or after June 7th 1873" indicates that the stockings, when knitted, would be taken to the hosier's warehouse. Pickering's book records a list of eleven warehouses in Hinckley in 1824 and one factory in Back Lane, now Factory Road A J Pickering, The Cradle and Home of the Hosiery Trade, Hinckley, 1945, p48.

1891 – In January of that year poverty in Hinckley was severe. Working hours were horrendously long, work was irregular, wages were pitiful and varied considerably from firm to firm. The Hinckley Times and Bosworth Herald (now the Hinckley Times) printed in an editorial "From what we hear there are startling discrepancies in the prices paid by the different firms in Hinckley. For one class of hose it differs from 2s 9d to 3s 9d and 4s 2d". In desperation the workers decided to form a Knitters' Union. The first secretary was a Leicester man with a proven record as a negotiator. The new union wrote up a "Standard Price List" to level up wages in the town. The Hinckley manufacturers threatened to close their factories rather than submit to the demands of the union and refused to acknowledge its secretary, Mr Holmes.

On Monday 13th April the strike began. By breakfast time every factory was empty, the workers were all now in the Union. Every firm in the town sent a

BROWN & GREY COTTON LIST (CIRCULAR).

Women's Brown Hose.

	s.	d.
Plain Welts, 2d. less — 2 striped welt, 1-0 to 2-8......	1	7½
" " — 2-12 and up ...	1	8½
Made Single 2d. extra — Nar. Toe Legs, 1-0 to 2-8......	1	6½
" — 2-12 and up ...	1	7½
Mock Seamed, 2-8..............	1	7½
" — 2-12 and up ...	1	8½
Nd. Heel or Guss. Legs, 2-8..............	1	6½
" 2-12	1	7½
Latch Needles Frames, Bro.	2	8
" Merino and Coloured	3	1

Boys' Brown Hose.

	s.	d.
Light Weights..................................	1	7
Heavy Weights	1	8
Made Single, 2d. extra — Narrow Toe, Light............	1	6
" Heavy	1	7
Mock Seamed, Light	1	7
" Heavy	1	8
Nar. Heel and Guss., Light	1	6
" " Heavy	1	7

Men's Brown Hose.

	s.	d.
Broad Stripe, 1d. less than Garters. .... 1-4 to 3-0......	1	8½
Garters, 1d. extra per score. .... 3-4 to 4-0......	1	9½
.... 4-4 to 5-0......	1	11
Single, 2d. extra. — Narrow Toe, Legs, 3-4 to 4-0......	1	8
" 4-4 to 5-0......	1	9
Mock Seamed, 3-4 to 4-0......	1	9
" 4-4 to 5-0......	1	10
Heelers made single, 3-4 to 4-0......	1	10
" " 4-4 to 5-0... ..	1	11
Latch Needles, Browns	2	8
" Coloured and Grey	3	1

Men's Grey Cotton Hose.

	s.	d.
Self Toes, ... 1-8 to 3-0......	2	2
" .... 3-4 to 4-8......	2	3
White Toes, ... 1-8 to 3-0......	2	4
" .... 3-4 to 4-8......	2	5
Single, 2d. extra. — Narrow Toe, Legs, all	2	2
Mock Seamed, Narrow Toe	2	3
Mock Seamed, Narrow Heel	2	2
Merino Mock Seamed, cut single	2	0

Boys' Grey Cotton Hose.

	s.	d.
Self Toes, ...Light	2	0
" ....Heavy.........	2	1
White Toes, ...Light	2	2
" ....Heavy	2	3
Single, 2d. extra. — Narrow Toes, ...Light	2	0
" ......Heavy.........	2	1
Mock Seamed, ...Light	2	1
" ...... Heavy.........	2	2
Mock Seamed, Narrow Gusset, Light	2	0
" " Heavy.........	2	1

White Merino and Brown Half-Hose.

	s.	d.
L.F., ...1-0 to 2-0.........		10
" ....2-1 to 2-12		11
Coloured Cotton, Grey, and Shetland Merino, ...1-0 to 2-0.........		11
..............2-4 to 2-12	1	0
Shoddy Yarns, ...1-0 to 2-0.........	1	0
" " ....2-4 to 2-12	1	1
Double lengths double price.		
Cleared Tops ....(Rotary)	4	2
" .... (Circular)......	4	7
Bag Feet Merino Half-Hose,		
Toes not Spliced... (Rotary)	3	4
(Circular Top)	3	9
" Spliced...... (Rotary)	3	9
" (Circular Top)	4	2
L. F., or Legs only, ...not Spliced	1	2
" " Striped or Spliced	1	3
" " Single	1	4
Cleared Tops, Striped		3½
Brown Cotton, White, Grey & Shet. Merino		
Cir. Tops, 5d. extra. — Half-Hose, N. T. Legs 2-0 ...	2	7
" " 2-4 ...	2	8
" " 2-8 ...	2	9
Gartered Socks	1	3
Mock Seamed 1d. extra.		
Circular Footing, Brown		1½
" " Coloured		2

Men's Grey Cotton Half-Hose.

	s.	d.
Self Toes, L. F., ...1-0 to 2-12	1	0
Cleared Tops .... (Rotary).........	4	5
" .... (Circular)......	4	10
White Toes, L. F., ...1-0 to 2-12	1	2
Cleared Tops .... (Rotary)...... ..	4	7
" .... (Circular)......	5	0

Men's Grey Cotton Half-Hose. *(continued)*

	s.	d.
Narrow Toes, 1-8 to 2-0	2	10
" 2-4 to 2-8	2	11
Mock Seamed 1d. extra, Jobbed on 5d. less.		

Stitching

	s.	d.
L. F. Hose		1
On Hague L. F. Half-Hose, turned, or not turned		1¼
On Patent Stitching Frame, not turned		1¼
" " " turned		1½
Cleared Top Half-Hose		1
Stitching Heels in		½
" Toes..		¼
" Loose Bottoms in		½
Toed Hose, Heels Linked		1
" " Stitched		1¼
" Half-Hose, with Tops Stitched on		1¾
Stitching Tops..		¼

Welting.

	s.	d.
Cup Machine, per 100 dozen	2	8
Patent, up to 3-0	2	9
" above 3-0..	2	10

Seaming.

	s.	d.
Not Turned, — On Rudolph & German Machines, Ft. 21o		1½
" " " " 24o		1¾
" " " " 30o		2
" " " Tops		½
" " " Heels		½
" " " Toes		¼
" " 24o and 30o "		¼
21o Wrought Half-Hose........................		2½
30o " Cotton		3¼
30o Wrought Merino		3½
Slits or Long Heels ½d. extra.		
Grey Cotton or White Toes ¼d. extra.		
Cuts, Spliced Ankle, ¼d. extra.		

Point Seaming.

	s.	d.
Feet		2½
Tops and Feet		3¼
Tops, Feet, and Heels..............................		3½
21o Wrought		4¼
24o "		4½
30o "		5
Cotton Striped		7
Merino		7½
If Linked ½d. less.		

Bag Heeling.

	s.	d.
On Circular Frames, job on		1½
Cleared, run on..		2

Linking.

	s.	d.
Fancys and Heathers, cut Heels	7	0
" " when on coarse machines	8	4
Fashioned Heels, pull through	6	3
Narrow Toe Hose and L. F. Half-Hose	6	3
" " Half-Hose, Toes and Heels......	5	0
Grey Cotton, Grey and Shetland Merino Hose, and Half-Hose Heels	6	3
Grey Cotton, and Grey Merino, Self......Toes	5	3
Brown, Shetland, and White Merino ... "	5	0
Coloured " " " "	6	0
Linking in Bottoms, White		1¼
" " Coloured		1½
Bag Feet Toes and Heels, both Narrowed ...		1½
" Narrow Heels, Cut Toes		1¾
" Cut " ditto		2
Linking on 30o tops		2½
(Rotary) Linking on Tops and Clearing......		1¾
" " " Dark		2
(Circular) " "		2½
26o work ¼d. extra.		

Circular Rib Tops.

	s.	d.
Pay for Needles, ¾d. each soldered, ½d. not soldered.		
One-feeder, Brown, White, Grey & Shetland		7
" Coloured		8
Welt and Slack Course, Brown, White, Grey and Shetland....................................		8
" " Coloured..............		9
If Tipped 1½d. extra.		
Two-feeder Frames, Brown, White, Grey and Shetland		5½
" Coloured		6½
If Cut 1d. extra per gross.		
Cutting Welted Tops, 2d. per gross.		

Warburton's Patent Winding.

	s.	d.
From 5 to 7½	1	8
" 8 to 10	2	1
" 11 to 14	2	4
" 15 to 24	3	3
Above 24/1 Winders to be Paid by Time.		

The above Prices having been mutually settled must be strictly adhered to. Any class of Work not arranged for on the List, to be submitted to the joint Committee of Employers and Workpeople.

Signed for the Manufacturers,
JNO. SMITH, Jun.,
WM. HURST,
C. A. MURCOTT, Secretary.

Signed for the Workpeople,
JOSEPH WARNER,
WILSON CHAPMAN,
JAMES HOLMES, General Secretary.

PICKERING, PRINTER, HINCKLEY.

representative to a meeting called for the purpose of forming a Hinckley Manufacturers' Association. The local newspaper reported "some effort must be made to prevent sheer starvation from falling upon unfortunate children and older persons who are without means of obtaining a bare existence".

On Monday 25th May came a breakthrough. A Hinckley man named Brookes, who had no connection with the hosiery trade, offered himself as a mediator. The Masters climbed down to the extent that the representatives of the Union should include Mr Holmes. The proposals concerning prices were gone through item by item. After a fortnight a list of prices was agreed and it seemed that the strike was at an end, but both sides found that the list of prices agreed had not completely set at rest the many issues involved. Some of the employers were dissatisfied with the prices they were expected to pay and refused to open their factories. The strike was on again. The difficult position was resolved by Mr Holmes. The newspaper commented "Mr Holmes has succeeded to an extent where hundreds of men would have failed". The final agreement meant that from that time the employers and employees would talk over any dispute as it occurred and marked the end of the terrible poverty that had existed and devastated the town for so long.

List of Prices Mutually Arranged June 10th 1891

The Price List was put up in every factory in Hinckley at the end of the strike. At the bottom of each list were the words "the above prices having been mutually settled must be strictly adhered to. Any class of work not on the List, to be submitted to the Joint Committee of Employers and Workpeople". The List was signed for the manufacturers by John Smith, junior, William Hurst and C A Murcott as Secretary. For the workpeople, it was signed by Joseph Warner, Wilson Chapman and James Holmes, the General Secretary. The List covered the following operations: circular hose, circular half hose, rotary, Cotton's patent hose and half hose, circular rib tops, shirts and pants, circular webbing, niantic footing, Griswold system, Warburton's patent winding, stitching, linking, seaming, point-seaming and welting. These prices added between 20% and 30% to the earnings of hosiery workers in Hinckley in 1891.

Kinship, Careers & Community - The Family Firms

Any survey of workers in the knitting and hosiery firms in Hinckley would show that in many, members of the same family, over several generations have been employed in the industry. This is true at all levels from directors, managers, mechanics and knitters to makers-up, finishers and packers. From oral and written testimonies given by former and existing hosiery workers, both proprietors and employees, it has been discovered that a large proportion of these people were introduced into the trade by family members. As well as finding continuity of ownership of "family" firms like Davenports, Bennetts, S Jennings Ltd, H J Hall and Son Ltd and until 1992, Atkins Brothers, it has also been noticed that some firms have employed several generations of the same family as production workers. As already seen, some of these families originate in the town from before enclosure in 1760. A good though undetermined proportion of those 350 families resident in the 1760's, deprived of their rights to use common land by enclosure, took up framework knitting as an occupation. Many of these original stockingers' descendants must still remain in the trade today. The Parish Registers, Poll Books, wills, inventories, leases, Rate and Property Valuations lists and trade directories show recurrent family names which are still common in the area and are represented by present day hosiery workers. Because of the diversification of surnames through maternal lines of descent and through women's marriage, actual name at present does not necessarily indicate descent. Looking back over generations a wide kinship network is revealed. What is significant about the documents (other than the Parish Registers) dating from or before enclosure is that those mentioned by name usually had property and rights associated with it This seems to have given them a head start in the developing industrial economy of the town. Many of the names of property owners from before and in 1760 are later recognised as hosiers and then later as factory owners. Robert Atkins for example received as compensation for loss of common rights associated with several cottages, a piece of land on Bond Street in central Hinckley which later became the site of the family's home, factory and the Unitarian chapel where they worshipped.

A long-lived firm was Daniel Payne and Son on Factory Road. When he married Sarah in 1854 (1), its founder Daniel Payne, married into the Hurst family (2) which, from legal documents, can be seen to have been hosiers as early as 1689 (3). Other members of the Payne family are recorded as having been a butcher, a shoe-maker and a tea-dealer but could also have been involved in the hosiery business as frame lenders. Daniel Payne's son, William Hurst Payne succeeded his father in the business. A family namesake of his, William Hurst was mentioned by name in the Enclosure Act. He gained a large piece of land behind the site of the castle in the Priesthills area, which became the family home. Hurst Road commemorates the family. A title deed relating to property on Stockwell Head which in 1772 was sold by Joseph Hurst, a framework knitter and son and heir of Joseph Hurst senior also a framework knitter, to John Brooks, a framesmith and John Boulton, a framework knitter. The heirs of Brooks, all named Boultbee Brooks continued in the trade of framesmith until at least 1865. John Brooks also bought land on King Street from the Hursts (4). From a will of 1784 not just Joseph Hurst but most of his immediate and extended family can be seen to have been in the trade at that time. He left a messuage to his cousin John Hurst of Ullesthorpe who was also a framework knitter as was

1 *Marriage Contract, Leicestershire Records Office*
2 *Bill Partridge, The Daniel Payne Story, Knitting International, February 1991, p88*
3 *William Hurst, hosier, was witness to the inventory of Samuel Ward in 1689 which is in Leicestershire Records Office*
4 *Title deeds relating to property in the Hinckley part of the Boultbee Brooks estate, 1772-1913, Leics Records Office, Acc no DE 3322*

another cousin, William who lived in Hinckley. Another knitter cousin, David Hurst inherited another messuage for life and then afterwards to his daughter for ever. He left a stocking frame to his cousin William, another to his cousin Mary Jackson, the wife of a knitter, one each to cousins Alice and Jane who were also the wives of framework knitters plus another one between them. His father Joseph's frame was left to another cousin, also called Joseph. Three of the frames were in the homes of other people one of them a widow named Sharpless, rented out to provide an investment and additional income. The Hursts were not only framework knitters themselves but hosiers renting out frames and probably putting out work as well (5). The Hursts and their descendants in the Payne family continued in the hosiery business until the twentieth century when Daniel Payne's factory closed in 1957.

The firm claiming to be the oldest existing firm in Hinckley was taken over by Coats-Viyella and renamed Counterpart in 1992. Until then it had been in the continuous ownership of the Atkins family since 1722. This family is descended from Robert Atkins (1665-1728) of Newbold on Avon, which is near Rugby in Warwickshire. He was a yeoman farmer with a large family that could not be supported from the proceeds of agriculture alone. The younger son of this farmer, also called Robert, left Newbold in 1715 to be apprenticed to a Brother of the Framework Knitters of London in Long Lawford (6), only a couple of miles from his home. Seven years later, free of his indentures, young Robert was making stockings in Hinckley only 12 miles or so away down Watling Street, the present day A5. This Robert Atkins was joined by his 20 year old nephew, yet another Robert Atkins in 1740. As master hosiers the business would have taken on apprentices, purchased and rented out frames, passed out raw materials to stockingers and collected and sold the finished products. This, according to the firm's own history, was the origin of the firm. Many other Hinckley firms started in the same way, and if investigated could probably prove to have just as ancient origins.

Atkins Factory now Counterpart, Hinckley

Most of the owners and some former owners of the main family firms in the town have helped provide information about their families for this publication. Using local directories such as Kelly's and Wright's listings of hosiery manufacturers from the years 1791 to 1923 and census returns from 1841 onwards as well as other documents available in the Records Office it is possible to build up knowledge of which families have been involved in the industry historically reaching back to the industrial revolution and before. Unfortunately the Enclosure Map for Hinckley, showing who had land and where, is missing. Sometimes the surviving documents are very difficult to read and understand and spelling is inconsistent. But by comparing these early records with early trade directories and rate books it is possible to see who had property and who is subsequently listed as a hosier.

Obviously the Enclosure Award, Poll Books and surviving legal documents are not a complete record of all Hinckley's inhabitants. Those who had no property rights such as labourers, servants and the unnamed majority were rarely explicitly mentioned. The study previously described of poor law records gives information about this less visible majority. Again some of

6 *The Atkins Story*

7 *Probate copy will of Joseph Hurst of Hinckley, framework knitter, Will 9 April 1784, proved 9 November 1791, Leicestershire Records Office, Acc no DE 3322/2*

these records go back to the late eighteenth century, almost to the time of enclosure. What these documents show are the names of existing framework knitters in the town who were taking on apprentices, again family involvement is shown by several people with the same family name involved in the trade. The names of their pauper apprentices show many of those who formed the initial influx into the town post-enclosure, in the first phase of industrial growth in the domestic system which was rapidly evolving into a workshop based industry. Sadly, these apprentices did not necessarily move to the town willingly but were sent by the poor law overseers in other parishes, affected by post-enclosure agrarian crisis in villages and small towns which did not industrialise at the same speed as Hinckley or concentrated on agrarian production. Again these records show that whole generations of the same family moved into the town as children, grew up in the hosiery trade and gained settlement, intermarrying with existing local residents, spreading the kinship network in the trade even wider. The same family names of both the framework knitters taking on apprentices and the apprentices themselves persist to the present, showing continuity from the past to the present. Despite a seeming lack of historic or ancient buildings, the real heritage of Hinckley is in its people.

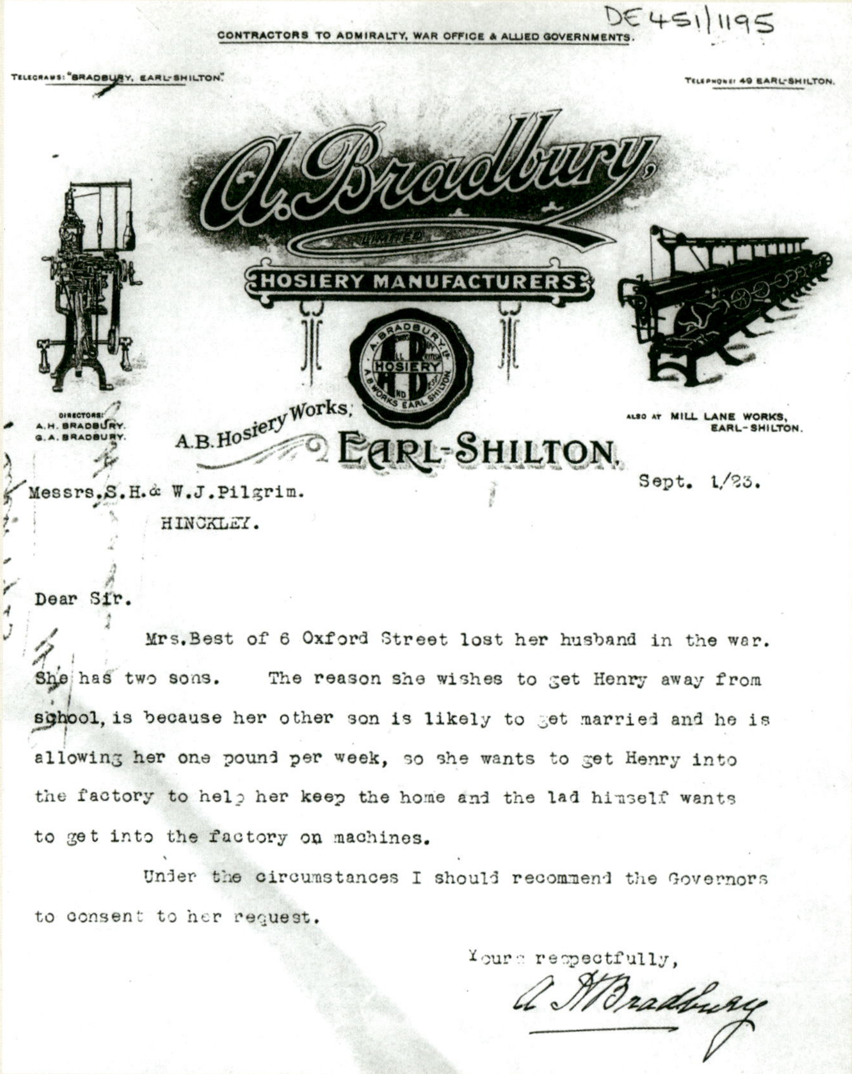
DE451/1195

CONTRACTORS TO ADMIRALTY, WAR OFFICE & ALLIED GOVERNMENTS.

TELEGRAMS: "BRADBURY, EARL-SHILTON." TELEPHONE: 49 EARL-SHILTON.

A. Bradbury, LIMITED

HOSIERY MANUFACTURERS

DIRECTORS: A.H. BRADBURY. G.A. BRADBURY.

A.B. Hosiery Works, EARL-SHILTON.

ALSO AT MILL LANE WORKS, EARL-SHILTON.

Messrs. S.H. & W.J. Pilgrim.
HINCKLEY.

Sept. 1/23.

Dear Sir.

Mrs. Best of 6 Oxford Street lost her husband in the war. She has two sons. The reason she wishes to get Henry away from school, is because her other son is likely to get married and he is allowing her one pound per week, so she wants to get Henry into the factory to help her keep the home and the lad himself wants to get into the factory on machines.

Under the circumstances I should recommend the Governors to consent to her request.

Yours respectfully,

A. H. Bradbury

The stories told by oral and written reminiscence respondents tell us that even at the end of the twentieth century, most hosiery and knitting workers have relatives in the trade. Many of these people were introduced to their jobs by other family members. Many interviewees describe how they were taken to the factory by older family members already working there to get their first job on leaving school, at 15 or 14 years of age. Others, with no relative in the factory, were introduced to work by family friends. Looking back many of them say they had no real choice of occupation, it was always assumed they would go into "the hosiery", often because their parents needed the money. Even those who had passed exams giving scholarships to grammar school were sometimes unable to take advantage of the opportunity offered because they were expected to contribute to the family income. This does not mean to say that young people were unwilling to go to work in the industry, just that they never really thought about any other kind of work. Until recently work in the hosiery industry was plentiful and well-paid for both males and females and it was the major employer in the town. Wages in the industry in the post World War II era were relatively high compared with other kinds of work.

From the early days of the household based domestic industry and frameshops, Hinckley's families have relied on a combined wage with women being economically active even with young children. Young people were required to make a contribution as soon as possible. Many oral testimonies emphasise that up until the 1960s wages of young workers were handed over to their mothers who would give back 2 shillings and sixpence (half a crown or some other amount) as pocket money. Although this opportunity for multiple income households was a source of relative prosperity during the first twenty-five years after the war when wages were relatively high, before this period it was a case of economic necessity and survival. Everyone had to contribute to the family income because of the otherwise prevailing poverty.

In the domestic system if family members were not available to undertake seaming and winding, the framework knitter would have to pay someone else to do it out of his payment from the hosier, thereby reducing the amount left for himself and his family. Child apprentices in the early industry fulfilled this role but as incomes fell fewer apprentices were taken on because of the expense of keeping them whether there was any work or not. The work then went to the knitter's own family. Formal education was not a priority for those children who were needed to work at home and couldn't be spared for full-

Women packers and male countermen, Manchester Hosiery, 1929

time schooling. Another problem was that they could not afford school or the clothes to wear to go in. In 1847 the only free school for poor children was provided by the Catholic and non-conformist churches, a fact that concerned some of members of the Church of England. In response to a circular issued by a committee of the proposed schools associated with Trinity Church in 1847, John Brown, a guardian, addressed the rate-payers of the parishes in the Hinckley Union. In it he said "that the poor of the town required food for the mind cannot for a moment be questioned. At the same time a great Christian duty points me to the startling fact that, a crisis has arrived when they also require food for the body" (7). In the Free Schools that were started, to encourage attendance, children were allowed to take stockings for seaming to school with them. Children sat sewing while they listened to their lessons giving rise to the name "seaming classes". (8) Workers in Hinckley were unlikely to have favoured the Education Act of 1870 which was to make elementary education compulsory nor the successive raising of the school leaving age. In the nearby Leicester and Bedworth areas school strikes in protest at the raising of the school leaving age happened with parental support in 1928-29. In this context, compulsory secondary education could be seen as an attack on working-class culture and living standards (9).

The mechanised factory system developed from the 1850s onwards led to an eventual decline in the numbers of male knitters but a high demand for women winders and then seamers, linkers and other machinists. This high number of women workers must have had social consequences such as the need to juggle domestic and factory work; the provision of childcare; greater financial independence for women and perhaps partnership rather than dependence in marriage; shopping habits relating to the convenience of produce purchased as well as opening hours. In Leicester, another hosiery town, oral reminiscences describe how shopkeepers prided themselves on the service they offered to their customers, many of whom were married women working in the hosiery factories. A bakery was described "as a sight to behold in the mornings, women going to work, you know, they'd got the baking tins with their dinner....(they'd) leave off at dinner time, come home, flying home... and she used to charge them 3d a day for cooking their dinners in the big ovens" (10). Other shops sold soaked peas by the pint, scraped potatoes, cooked bacon and hot soup. Women working in factories took great pride in their ability to contribute to the household income. They were known for having nice homes and well kept children. One employer interviewed for this project said that in the past most women worked full-time even after motherhood but nowadays many preferred to work part-time. This may reflect changing

7 *John Brown, An Address to the Rate-payers of the Several Parishes Comprised in the Hinckley Union, 1847*
8 *Pickering, p64*
9 *Stephen Humphries, Hooligans or Rebels? An Oral History of Working-class Childhood, Oxford, 1981*
10 *Cynthia Brown, Wharf Street Remembered, Leicester Living History Unit, 1997*

standards in childcare or lack of communal or family support networks for families. Despite family involvement in hosiery, it is now unusual for workers, even those who enjoy their work, to say that they would encourage their own children to enter the trade. Nowadays expectations are higher and there is more choice of job because of diversification in the local economy.

This lack of career choice didn't just affect the workers but factory owners representing several generations in the business also felt under obligation to carry on the family trade. At Atkins' twenty-two family members worked in the business between 1722 and 1992. Tom Atkins of the last but one generation to work in the firm, who retired soon after it was taken over by Coats-Viyella, in an interview said that he had wanted to be a farmer but, understandably, the family wanted him to be in the business. After six months with the firm he joined the Marines and a family row broke out over it. Later Tom's military career became incorporated into the needs of the firm when he became a reservist in Bristol and at the same time West Country sales manager.

This is not an isolated example. David Jennings, another inheritor of a family business, would also have liked to have been a farmer but his father expected him to go into industry. There were other practical problems to his ambition. National Service was compulsory as well as which two years of agricultural experience was required before getting in at Brooksby agricultural college. Another important consideration was that in farming the pay was only £7 a week compared with £35 a week in industry.

John Bennett wanted to join the navy but couldn't get in to do the job in which he was interested. However, he was under no pressure to join the firm. His own son as well as a brother was now working in the business. Another younger director at Davenports said he always expected to go into the family business and never really considered any alternative until after he was there. Neville Hall of H J Socks said it was assumed that he would join the business as soon as possible at the age of about 17. However, he would prefer his own children to wait until they were 25 or more with some outside experience before joining the family business, should they wish do to so.

It is emphasised here that no one has said that they regret joining the business. It is quite usual for people to think retrospectively about other careers even if they are happy in their work.

Employers share a number of things in common. In the generation of grandparents early in the century, most were educated locally at the Grammar School, itself quite a privilege in the days before universal free secondary education. By the 1930s sons were mostly privately educated and went to boarding school after preparatory school or a local private school. This tradition continues into the present generation. What is different now is that previous generations usually went to technical college to learn the practicalities of knitting and the associated technologies, usually in Leicester in what is now de Montfort University or initially to Hinckley Technical College, now the Hinckley site of the North Warwickshire and Hinckley College. Younger members of owner families now tend to go to university before entering the business and may not necessarily study a subject which is directly relevant, learning management and manufacturing skills later.

Successive generations of Hinckley manufacturers have exercised a degree of either paternalism or social control depending on the point of view. Individual members of the Victorian generations of the Atkins family, for example, founded the public library in memory of a deceased brother, were on the committee of the local hospital, were founding governors of the town's technical college, founded the operatic society, were Unitarian chapel benefactors, administrators of a charitable trust to provide coal for the elderly poor, captains of local cricket and rugby teams, a master of the Atherstone Hunt, a Justice of the Peace, secretary of the Mechanics' Institute and local councillors. This commitment to local initiatives and to the community was also true of many other employer families like the Halls, Davenports, Bennetts and Jennings. These activities were shared with other hosiers, the employers would therefore have spent quite a lot of time together. It is difficult in earlier eras to see how they had time to do any work. Presumably much of the day to day running of the businesses was done by professional managers, an occupation that arose in the late Victorian years. Public institutions important to the civic and cultural life of the community were originally controlled or financed

T Jennings & Son former factory on Upper Bond Street, Demolished 1998

HINCKLEY MECHANICS' INSTITUTE.

President---THE EARL HOWE.

Vice-President—CHARLES NOEL, ESQ.

THE COMMITTEE of the above Institution have to inform the Working-men of the Town and Neighbourhood that they have taken (at some considerable expense) the Friends' Meeting-house, in Castle-street, for the better accommodation of the Members, which is opened every day from nine in the morning till ten at night (Sundays excepted).

The table of the Reading-room is supplied with the following Nespapers and Periodicals, viz.:—*The Express* (daily), *Leicestershire Mercury, Coventry Herald, Birmingham Advertizer, The Alliance, Punch, London Journal, and Cassell's Illustrated Paper ; Blackwood, Tait, Dickens's Houshold Words and Narrative, Chambers' Journal, Musical Times*, &c., &c.

CLASSES, for reading, writing, and arithmetic, are held every Monday and Tuesday Evenings, at eight o'clock, under the superintendence of Mr Green and Mr Greatorex, and Vocal Music, on Thursday Evening.—All of which advantages, together with free admission to Lectures and Concerts, added to a Library of 300 volumes, are available to the Working Classes, on payment of ONE PENNY per week.

The age in which we live is characterized as much by its achievements in literature and art, as in those of war. The time has arrived, so much talked of in the world's history, when intellectual culture is within the reach of every man, and he who neglects to gather its fruits, neglects his own welfare : for it has been proved, agreeable to Lord Bacon's dictum, That " Knowledge is Power." —That the giving increased Knowledge to the head, neither paralizes the hand nor the foot.—That in manual labour it is even more effective than brute force, and as men rise in the scale of intelligence, they become better workmen—better parents—better in every relation of life.

From the necessitous condition of a large portion of the population of our Town, Children are taken at a very early age from school. What they *can* acquire there, it should be born in mind, is but a very small part of what *ought* to be the Education of the people ; and, hence the necessity,—not only in youth but in after life—*that all* should have within their reach the means of further development.

Who has not had their ears offended by the noisy mirth and obscenity which rings through our streets, during the leisure hours of evening ? and, Who has not lamented the moral pestilence which is thereby created around us ? The best preservative against evil is employment in good.—Thus by bringing our youth under better influences—by taking them from the street to the class-room—with the same rapidity, that they learn, from evil communications, bad manners, would they imitate good ones.

Society is constituted of various classes, differing in rank and station—Some are born to riches, some to power, some to govern, and some to be governed. Some belong to the " aristocracy of intellect," while others inherit mental imbecility, and from causes entirely independent of themselves. An equality of condition, therefore, however specious and beautiful in theory, is perfectly Utopian,—a mere incubus of political enthusiasts, which vanishes before the light of Reason. The Working-man has as many sources of solid content and rational pleasure as his employer, if he will but use them ; and may be, if it is not his own fault, as great an object of respect and esteem amongst his fellows ; but, unfortunately, in our old Town, this social concord is lamentably confused—We forget, that in the welfare of the whole consists that of its parts—And that this discordance, can alone be harmonized on a *truly* catholic ground.

A MECHANICS' INSTITUTE affords such a basis, and should be a kind of magnet, drawing all to one point, from which will radiate a common good—Teaching persons of various creeds and opinions, the great duty of mutual forbearance and respect— of mutual toleration, good-will, and charity.

JOHN ATKINS, Hon. Sec.

25 September, 1854.

(Burgess, Printer.)

Hosiers involved themselves in a range of social and community activities.

by hosiers, using of course money produced from the work of their employees. It would be true to say that modern Hinckley was built by the knitting community and the wealth it created. Even now, college and school governing bodies have a representation of knitting manufacturers. Parks and public space were donated by hosier benefactors, even the working-men's club is in the former home of the Atkins family and the Hinckley Co-operative Society in its early days had a lot of involvement from members of hosiery families such as Flude, Davenport, Jennings and Bolesworth, in the trade themselves and predecessors of future knitwear businessmen.

Where the family involvement of factory owners differs from that of workers is in the area of gender involvement. While women workers have been employed in large numbers in seaming, linking, design, overlocking and nowadays even in management alongside male knitters, mechanics and managers, the family firms are all controlled by male heirs. The only exeptions found so far are a Victorian widow and mother of the Atkins Brothers who moved into factory production, a Flude widow who looked after the business before her son was old enough to take over and a younger woman of the present day working at T Jennings tights manufacturers. However, women have received shares, often on a equal basis with their brothers. Even though they have no involvement with the running of the firms, they benefit financially or have done so because of the educational and social opportunities the business has been able to buy for them.

In the past hosier employers often married into other hosiery manufacturing families. In the twentieth century where this has happened it seems to be coincidental. What employer family spouses do have in common is that they have usually come from families themselves in trade. In the early part of the twentieth and in the nineteenth century, they were often daughters of shopkeepers, if not hosiers themselves. Nowadays partners are often business or professional people in their own right.

When studying hosiery firms, those investigated still exist or have only recently demised. This may give a false impression of prosperity and security. We know about those that have survived but it is harder to learn about firms that didn't. In a study of Nottingham it was seen that there was a lot of fluidity of people coming into and out of the business with a great number of bankruptcies. The long-lived Hinckley firms may be the exception to the norm. In Nottingham, more men who began their careers as manual workers or over-lookers were to be found in the early days of the factory system than in any subsequent period. Nearly all these framework knitters, frame-smiths and craftsmen founded their own firms as family enterprises without any supplementary partners to provide capital or business experience. They hired one or two rooms in a powered building but were not on the whole successful in founding firms that survived them. It seems that those firms that did survive were set up by merchant hosiers with capital behind them, made in the manual trade from frame rents or workshop production (11). From the small sample looked at in Hinckley this seems also to have been the case in the town. By looking back beyond this it would seem that the inheritance of property rights acquired before and through enclosure or the ability to acquire them in the immediately ensuing period and the continuation of an existing business in the manual trade was important as it gave back up resources and access to finance while the new factory based business got going. In the 1860's and 1870's new firms had a higher death rate than merchant hosiery houses, at least in Nottingham, where four out of five of the old merchant firms survived over 30 years after moving to a factory. Of the new concerns less than a third lasted for 30 years.

In Hinckley the partnership agreements creating jointly owned companies show that community and kinship had an important influence on the early development of businesses. Partnerships seem to have been created, dissolved and re-created in different combinations fairly frequently before a stable business relationship seems to have been firmly established. Some partnerships dissolved because the partners wanted to bring in family members as new partners or formed new relationships, not because the business failed as the same names occur in future partnerships. Jennings, Wills and Herbert went into partnership in 1892 with a share capital of £1,100 made up of £400 from Mr Jennings, £420 from Mr Wills and £280 from Mr Herbert. In 1894 the trio increased their investments, Mr Jennings' share went up to £420, Mr Wills' contribution was £440 while Mr Herbert's share increased more substantially to £410. In 1904 Mr Wills retired, such was the success of his investment £733 was returned to him as the value of his share of the business (12). The remaining pairing of Jennings and Herbert had their partnership dissolved in 1907. S W Jennings continued in business until recently.

Arthur Davenport and Joseph Ginns dissolved their partnership in 1894 when Mr Davenport went into a new venture. The stock and effects of this company were worth £400 and there was a mortgage of £1,100. For his share of the business Mr Davenport received £700 on retiring from the partnership. Joseph Ginns took over the mortgage with Thomas Goodman, a builder and carried on with the business himself. That same year Davenport and Miles the short-lived partnership between Arthur Davenport, of Hinckley and Brydon Minion Miles, a hosier of Atherstone in north Warwickshire was agreed. Established with share capital of £700 from each partner, the joint business lasted only six months. Mr Davenport was to receive two-thirds of the profits and Mr Miles one-third. Both men were to work in the business and be paid £1 10s per week. After the dissolution of the partnership, Mr Davenport returned to Mr Miles his investment and carried on running the business, which had not failed but had been ended by a free decision, himself. Out of these dissolved partnerships emerged Ginns, Son and Moore in 1898 and A Davenport and Sons. Ginns Son and Moore was a partnership between Robert Ginns, presumably the son of Joseph Ginns and Joseph Moore. At the time they joined the trade, their factory and stock was worth £1,897 with a surplus capital of £341 17s divided between them at £150 15s 6d to Robert Ginns and £191 1s 6 to Joseph Moore. They both worked full time in the business.

Wileman and Simpkin joined together in 1872, the terms of their partnership agreement changing in 1874. The partnership was between Richard Wileman of Hinckley, a manufacturer, Joseph Simpkin of Narborough, styled gent, and Samuel John Simpkin of Narborough, a manufacturer. Wileman held a half share in the business and until the terms of their agreement altered in 1877, £200 extra out of the profits. The two Simkins held a quarter share each. Wileman was to be paid £400 a year, Joseph Simpkin £150 and Samuel £50 per year. The amount received by each partner altered after 1877 to eight-twelfths of the profit to Wileman, three-twelfths to Joseph Simpkin and one-twelfth to Samuel Simpkin. By 1881 the firm of Simpkin, Son and Smith was in existence and soon Simpkin Son and Emery on the site of the earliest factory in the town to be described as such on Factory Road and Upper Bond Street (13).

Excell machines, used at H.J. Hall & Sons, HInckley, formerly of Stoke Golding for knitting socks.

11 Charlotte Ericson, British Industrialists - Steel and Hosiery 1850-1950, Cambridge, 1959, p187

12 Articles of partnership and deeds of dissolution, LRO DE451

13 Pickering, p51

Samuel Davis brought his son, Sam, into his business in 1882 by making him a partner in his factory or warehouse as it was described in the deed, the property and stock being worth £14,886. This was the capital for the new partnership; Sam was to bring in no capital himself but would be paid £200 per year. Sam was to work in the business and in no other without his father's consent. The father, Samuel, was to put in whatever time he thought fit and have other business interests if he wished. He could also bring in one or two other sons as partners if he wished to do so. In January 1891 Harry John Davis became a partner. In November of 1891 the Davis's were joined by Arthur Taylor in their business which was valued at £29,608 1s 8d. Taylor invested capital of £207 12s 6d. Samuel Davis, the father, was to be paid £300 a year by the firm and his sons and Arthur Taylor were to receive £25 per month each, a high wage in 1891. Only Samuel, the father, was allowed to sign company cheques. Another son, Arthur Lancelot Davis, became a partner in 1896 when the value of the business had fallen to £24,98418s 3d.

An older hosiery business based in a factory belonged to John Flavell. In 1849 the 29 year old John had married 23 year old Louisa Culver Smith. When her husband died, Louisa Flavell inherited his business that included a factory, engine and boiler. A house was situated within the site of the factory. The widow does not seem to have wanted to run the firm herself and in 1868 she went into partnership with members of her own family, presumably her brothers. The partnership comprised John Cooper Smith, Alfred Cooper Smith and Louisa Flavell. Mrs Flavell's share of the business was £1,200 and that of the Smiths £1,000 each. The Smiths were to manage the business and be paid £1 10s each weekly plus a share in the profits of no more than £100 per year. Mrs Flavell was to receive £150 per year and £100 rent for the factory.

Lack of continuity in the same firm does not prove lack of continuity in the industry. New firms were sometimes founded by people who had been involved in other firms. An example would be Hall and Sons, H J Socks, set up in 1882 by a former foreman at Atkins with capital supplied by savings and his wife's property. Fludes is a more recent firm founded in 1926 as a partnership between Harry Flude and his brother-in-law W Collins, who sadly died in the same year. Harry Flude continued in the firm until his death in 1946 when his widow, together with a manager, Joe Warner, carried on the business until his son could come into the business himself in 1951. Harry was perhaps new to self-owned factory production in 1926 but there are many previous records of Fludes in Hinckley going back to the early 1800's. Most of them were framework knitters. Life was not always prosperous for the Flude family,

W F Wade in Office, 1929
Manchester Hosiery Mfg Co Ltd, Queens Road, Hinckley

they were affected by the prevailing hardships of Victorian Hinckley along with the rest of the community. Fludes appear in poor law records and one of them was arrested for his involvement in poaching a hare. Solomon Flude, who Francis described as one of the oldest inhabitants of Hinckley in 1930, related to the town's co-operative society in 1911, how he distinctly remembered his father and mother in about 1860 working hard at their frames early and late, even staying up the whole of Friday night to make only as much as 10 shillings for the week between them (14). Before going into business with his brother-in-law, Harry Flude had worked at T Jennings' factory.

Another long established Hinckley firm is the Manchester Hosiery Manufacturing Company Limited which was founded in 1906, with William Wade, who was a boot sewer, John Harris who was a boot manufacturer and William Hipwell, who was a hosiery manufacturer forming a partnership with three Lancashire cotton manufacturers. Initially Mr Hipwell was managing director but later Mr Wade succeeded him. William Wade's sons, followed him into the business. The firm remained under the directorship of the Wade family until 1986 when they sold the family business to a new consortium (15).

Before the factory epoch, families and individuals supplemented other trades or occupations by framework knitting and if they had any cash to spare invested it in the purchase of additional frames which could be rented out as an additional source of income. This may explain why some families known to have been in the trade were sometimes listed in trade directories not as hosiery manufacturers but as public house keepers, grocers or other types of shopkeepers.

Some sons did not carry on in the father's business but left to set up on their own. For example earlier in the twentieth century James Bennett's son Clive carried on in the firm but Clive's brother set up another company in Hinckley called Tudor Rose. Their own sons are now employed in the business as are their grandsons. The Davenport family are not all involved in the same firm but have two separate companies. Although the firm dates back to Victorian times, the present director's grandfather had a firm and four sons. Three of them went into the company but the fourth set up on his own forty years ago. The original firm has now sold up but the newer one carries on. There have now been five generations of Davenports running Hinckley hosiery factories.

David Jennings' firm T Jennings Ltd, was established by his grandfather and his three sons in 1918. Grandfather Timothy Jennings was previously in partnership as Jennings and Bolesworth but the partnership was dissolved so that he could take his sons into the business. Timothy had been a knitter at Atkins before the partnership and had married the sister of S W Jennings another, unrelated, hosiery manufacturer. David's own father had trained as a plumber before giving it up to join the business. His cousins, nephew and daughter are all involved in the firm. Timothy Jennings' partner Mr Bolesworth was a member of an old Hinckley family with pre-enclosure roots in the community. The family had been involved in the trade since then as hosiers and framework knitters and partners in other businesses. The family name also appears regularly working in other factories.

This family involvement has made Hinckley quite a tight knit community which may be supportive for those who are part of it but which can also serve a conservative function. If the majority find work through family connections, how can an outsider find a job in the trade? Despite the numbers of Asian people, many with experience in the hosiery and knitting trades, living in nearby Nuneaton and Leicester, very few employees of Asian origin seem to work in the local factories.

A lot of networking takes place within the trade to get the required capacity to meet large orders on time. Many of the last generation of employers were freemasons. At shop floor level networking to get jobs was and still is important. David Jennings confirmed that most of his employee's families are also in the trade. He describes Hinckley people as bred into the industry which needs a lot of skill and dexterity, for example a female toe-stitcher will make 24,000 repetitions of the same operation a week to make 1,000 dozen pairs of tights, each of which contains eight miles of yarn.

Jennings and Son Ltd

14 *Hinckley and District Industrial Co-operative Society Limited, A Brief History of its Rise and Progress, 1861-1911, published as a souvenir of its fiftieth anniversary, Hinckley 1911, p4*

15 *Information sheet produced by Manchester Hosiery Manufacturing Company Limited*

Factory Life

"A Factory Up Every Entry"

An industrial landscape showing factory chimneys and terraced housing. 1929. (Hinckley Times)

During its long involvement in the hosiery industry, Hinckley has experienced many changes with both booms and slumps in the economy of the town, and the prosperity of its people, as a result of fluctuations in trade. Sadly, like many other industries in the late twentieth century, hosiery is affected by world-wide economic recession. However, A J Pickering rightly describes Hinckley as the "Cradle and Home of the Hosiery Trade"(1); William Iliffe having brought the stocking frame to Hinckley in 1640 about forty years before it was introduced to Leicester. As stated in a trade directory of 1854 "...with the exception of Leicester, this is the largest manufacturing town in the county". (2) The manufacture of hose has been the staple industry of the town for well over two centuries, although this has gradually given way to increased manufacture of other knitted goods which are taken here as included under the general description of hosiery.

One of the prominent features of Hinckley town centre is the proliferation of jitties and yards which developed as the town expanded from a small farming community in the seventeenth century to a town whose wealth and prosperity depended on the hosiery and knitwear industry, with its numerous factories found in every street. This legacy is described vividly by Mr Evans who came into Hinckley from Stockingford to work at Bennett Brothers in 1934, "*....they had a factory up about every entry, a hosiery factory up about every entry. Hundreds of them!*". Many of these factories still survive and are still in the business of manufacturing hosiery and knitwear today and as observed by Marilyn Palmer in 1984 "The town of Hinckley in Leicestershire probably preserves the typical industrial landscape of the steam-powered hosiery production better than anywhere else in the East Midlands".(3)

This chapter portrays the continuity of family involvement in the hosiery industry over the years and describes individual people's involvement in the industry, wages earned, introduction to the workplace and types of jobs. This has been achieved by focusing on discussions, oral interviews, written accounts and completed questionnaires, but also includes information from earlier sources, where necessary, to bring alive the history of those involved in the hosiery

Mansion Street and Lower Bond Street with Bott and Son in the background. Pre 1914. (Hinckley Times)

1 - A.J.Pickering, Cradle and Home of the Hosiery Trade 1640-1940, Hinckley, 1940
2 - Melville and Company, Directory and Gazetteer. 1854
3 - Marilyn Palmer, Framework Knitting, Shire Album 119, 1984, p. 28

industry in the local area. Those who have participated have ranged from Managing Directors to supervisors, linkers, knitters, mechanics, folders, baggers and so on (past and present) and thus a fascinating insight into the local community has emerged.

It is possible to create an intimate picture of the local community from the late nineteenth century to the present day from the memories of the sixty or so people who have volunteered information for the research project. These people have drawn on recollections of their own experiences and the lives of parents and grandparents and have thus contributed to painting a vivid picture of factory life in the town and surrounding villages during this period. For instance, Mrs Pegg's grandfather worked as a stoker at Bradbury's in Earl Shilton, "*...and people who worked at Bradbury's used to go down to grandma's for their hot water to mash their teas*". This apparently inconsequential comment is in fact one of many which gives an indication of the communal significance and involvement of the local people in the hosiery and such recollections should not be ignored. By compiling an oral archive, life in all its diversity is made visible, a way of life which would not otherwise be recorded. The comings and goings of ordinary working people are made accessible by using the medium of a tape recorder. In "The Handbook of Oral History", Stephen Humphries tells us that "Oral history draws upon the memories of people whose experiences have often been neglected and excluded from history books..." (4)

Continuity of family involvement in the hosiery industry from one generation to the next has been highlighted, amongst others, by Mr Simpson who started work as a mechanic at Atkins in 1948 where, incidentally, his father worked as a knitter. He recalls:

> *"My grandmother Swan during the First World War was a staunch Wesleyan chapel person and my mother used to tell me that my great aunts and my grandmother used to sit in the kitchen - I can see the kitchen now - with an old stone copper built in the corner and they had large tables with Griswold hand machines - sock machines.....and they were producing the army greys. They used to belt these out with the heels and toes and when the bundles were made-up my mother used to carry these bundles up to the factory - believe it was Keen and Phelps in Earl Shilton - to have the heels and toes linked up and sent off to the forces in France".*

This picture of family continuity is further emphasised by Miss Smart. She started work in the hosiery at the age of fourteen in 1944 and recalls the involvement of her brothers, sisters, parents, aunts and uncles in the industry. Her mother worked until giving up her job in Davenport's factory in 1930 on giving birth to Miss Smart, her fourth child, after which, "*She never went out to work again*". However, the inter-dependence of employees and the manufacturing families was not easily broken and her mother subsequently:

> *"Started doing a bit of cleaning and what-not for Mrs Davenport across the road, who was the grandmother of the present hosiery manufacturer, you see".*

This highlights a community which many would agree was *"close knit"* with both employee and employer traditionally working and often living in close proximity to each other. The boss's house in the early days of factory production would often be situated next to his factory. John Hall, for instance, built his house adjacent to his hosiery business in Stoke Golding; while members of the Atkins family lived in a house on Lower Bond Street which adjoined their factory. Manufacturers often had very substantial houses built in the town, reflecting their increasing prosperity over the years. Many of these properties have now been converted to other uses such as hotels and nursing homes.

Grandfather Ellis. A framework knitter. (K Lockton)

Employees pose for a group photograph. Mr Harry Flude on right hand side. Mid 1930s. (Flude Hosiery)

4 *Stephen Humphries, The Handbook of Oral History - Recording Life Stories, London, 1984, p. ix*

Mrs Godfrey (sitting at the back) started her working life as a splicer and went on her own machine at 15 as a welter (M Godfrey)

Family involvement in the hosiery is ever present in the recorded discussions with respondents and Mr Smith who began his working life at the age of fifteen in 1955, speaks about his family and in particular about his Uncle Charlie and Uncle George:

> *"Uncle Charlie, he was one of the old firm, 'cause when he was a youngster, he used to fetch one of the old, original Atkins bosses. He used to live at The Manor, as it is now. That was one of the Atkins houses. He used to go down in the mornings with the pony and trap and bring him to work, when he was about twelve, thirteen. That was one of his jobs".*

Uncle George, though not employed in the hosiery trade, also had dealings with the Atkins family. He was a cobbler -

> *"...the old fashioned cobbler. He used to make the shoes for the Atkins bosses, riding boots, they were all big horsy-hunt people. And one of them was a cripple so he had to have boots specially made. Uncle George used to make them for him. I always used to watch him in his trade at the time, he used to live about three doors from us. And in the front room of the house, he had his cobbler's shop - it was amazing, we used to watch him. A piece of leather, a mouthful of nails - amazing".*

Respondents have spoken entertainingly about their introduction into the industry. More often than not jobs would be waiting for them when they left school. Mothers, fathers, aunties, uncles, friends would *"put a good word in"* for these young people. Mrs Read, who started work in the mid 1940s, remembers her introduction to working life quite vividly:

> *"In them days, you know, you'd know you'd got to go to work. So anyway, I'd got an aunty - any elderly aunty that worked at Minards: 'Oh!' she said, 'There's a job going up Minards. They want somebody to learn the mending'. I said 'I'm coming up aunty'. 'Just come into me', she said, 'And then I'll take you to see Mr. Minard'. He was elderly, he were nice, old Mr. Minard were. 'You want a job do you me duck', he said".*

The influence of family is still evident today, albeit to a lesser degree. A shift foreman at Flude Hosiery refers to the existence of *"A certain nepotism - we all look after each other"*. Mrs Evans, who started work at James Bennett Ltd in the mid 1970s, speaks of how her dad, who knew one of the Directors at the factory, got her a job *"And that's usually how we all work 'cause it's a small company and everybody knows everybody. And a lot of people on the shop floor we know from school"*. Family and community involvement in the industry has benefited both employer and employee over the years. These people knew each other and recruiting future employees by word-of-mouth was influential in building up "a core of long-serving workers". (5) And indeed many would say that the hosiery is *"in-bred"* in the local community, skills being passed down from one generation to the next. Quite a few respondents have worked for the same manufacturer all their working lives which adds up to typically fifty-one years for men and forty-six years for women if they started work at fourteen, as was often the case. Mr Lawrance moved from Bradbury's in Earl Shilton to Halls of Stoke Golding in 1938 as a young mechanic in his mid twenties. He watched Mr Neville Hall, now the Managing Director, grow up but also remembers well Mr Hall's father and grandfather. Although he did not start his working life at Hall's he, nevertheless, believes long service to one company leads to a sense of loyalty to the firm. Sadly he now feels that loyalty and respect from the employee has all but disappeared. But

A hive of activity. "If the belt stopped everything stopped" Mr James Bennett's factory 1927. (I. Milton)

5 David Nash and David Reeder, *Leicester in the Twentieth Century*, Leicester, 1993, p.171

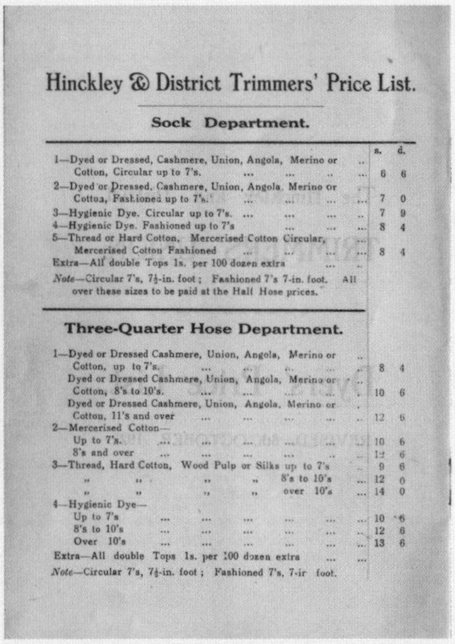

Hinckley & District Trimmers' Price List.

Sock Department.

	s.	d.
1—Dyed or Dressed, Cashmere, Union, Angola, Merino or Cotton, Circular up to 7's.	6	6
2—Dyed or Dressed, Cashmere, Union, Angola, Merino or Cotton, Fashioned up to 7's.	7	0
3—Hygienic Dye. Circular up to 7's.	7	9
4—Hygienic Dye. Fashioned up to 7's	8	4
5—Thread or Hard Cotton, Mercerised Cotton Circular, Mercerised Cotton Fashioned	8	4
Extra—All double Tops 1s. per 100 dozen extra		

Note—Circular 7's, 7½-in. foot; Fashioned 7's 7-in. foot. All over these sizes to be paid at the Half Hose prices.

Three-Quarter Hose Department.

	s.	d.
1—Dyed or Dressed Cashmere, Union, Angola, Merino or Cotton, up to 7's.	8	4
Dyed or Dressed Cashmere, Union, Angola, Merino or Cotton, 8's to 10's.	10	6
Dyed or Dressed Cashmere, Union, Angola, Merino or Cotton, 11's and over	12	6
2—Mercerised Cotton—		
Up to 7's.	10	6
8's and over	12	6
3—Thread, Hard Cotton, Wood Pulp or Silks up to 7's	9	6
" " " " 8's to 10's	12	0
" " " " over 10's	14	0
4—Hygienic Dye—		
Up to 7's	10	6
8's to 10's	12	6
Over 10's	13	6
Extra—All double Tops 1s. per 100 dozen extra		

Note—Circular 7's, 7½-in. foot; Fashioned 7's, 7-in foot.

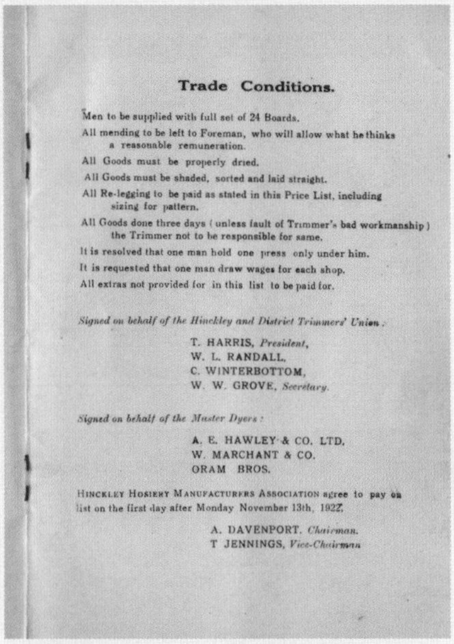

Trade Conditions.

Men to be supplied with full set of 24 Boards.

All mending to be left to Foreman, who will allow what he thinks a reasonable remuneration.

All Goods must be properly dried.

All Goods must be shaded, sorted and laid straight.

All Re-legging to be paid as stated in this Price List, including sizing for pattern.

All Goods done three days (unless fault of Trimmer's bad workmanship) the Trimmer not to be responsible for same.

It is resolved that one man hold one press only under him.

It is requested that one man draw wages for each shop.

All extras not provided for in this list to be paid for.

Signed on behalf of the Hinckley and District Trimmers' Union:

T. HARRIS, *President*,
W. L. RANDALL,
C. WINTERBOTTOM,
W. W. GROVE, *Secretary*.

Signed on behalf of the Master Dyers:

A. E. HAWLEY & CO. LTD.
W. MARCHANT & CO.
ORAM BROS.

HINCKLEY HOSIERY MANUFACTURERS ASSOCIATION agree to pay on list on the first day after Monday November 13th, 1922.

A. DAVENPORT, *Chairman*.
T JENNINGS, *Vice-Chairman*

The Hinckley and District Trimmers' Union. Price List. Revised 6th October 1922 (J Lawrance)

loyalty works both ways and a number of respondents have spoken about outsiders being brought into managerial positions in more recent years. These they refer to as *"whizz kids"* who they suggest know nothing about the industry or indeed the people with whom they work!

Neville Evans, born and bred in Nuneaton, recalls his mother's influence in his choice of job, " *'Me lad', she said, '...go to Hinckley', she says, 'you'll have to work hard'* . *But she used to say 'It's the hardest penny you'll earn but it's good money'* ". Mr Evans started work in the 1930s when depression had hit large areas of the country, the North East and South Wales in particular. Though the Midlands escaped the worst ravages of the depression and the hosiery industry in the east Midlands remained relatively boyant, many people did experience unemployment and short time work. Trade Directories show the population of Hinckley as increasing from 9,600 in 1900 to 32,000 by 1941 with a corresponding increase in Hosiery Manufacturers from 25 to over 50. (6) The number of shop floor workers involved in the production of hosiery in the local area by 1939 was approximately 7,500 (7).

A job in the hosiery was more often than not accepted by the majority of school leavers. However, a number of respondents have spoken about how they or family members who, under different circumstances, would have followed other occupations if family fortunes and parents had allowed. Miss Coley, who started work at the age of thirteen in 1917 at Norton and Bradbury in Earl Shilton, has spoken of her mother's dependence on her weekly wage: she was a widow and every penny her children earned was essential to the family budget. Miss Coley *"turned-up"* her wage to her mother until she was twenty-three Another respondent has talked about her brother and sister: both were extremely bright but there was not enough money to allow them to attend the local grammar school. The following highlights a parent's influence over their child's future: *"My school report said suitable for office work, but parents took you straight to the factory. I had a relative married to the Moore's* (hosiery manufacturers) *that's why I got took on. Office went for a burton!"*.

As discussed by Mrs Hall who started work in the mid 1950s, there was often little choice of employment. Hosiery was the dominant industry in the town and it drew girls and women from the surrounding areas and as she says *"It was deemed as a good job, you see"*.

By 1959 local membership of the National Union of Hosiery Workers totalled 5,335 of which 3,455 were women. (8) A characteristic of the hosiery and knitwear industry since the advent of the factory system has been the dominance of female workers and an often strict demarcation between male and female work has existed. Overlocking, lockstitching, splicing, mending, welting and linking are examples of typical female jobs on the factory floor. Male jobs include for example, mechanics, trimmers, dyers and knitters. However, female knitters

"It was common in those early days to dye cotton stockings in open vats, sometimes fitted with a paddle to rotate the goods through the liquor." (B. Hall)
Dye House, 1930s, Bennett Brothers. (B. Partridge)

6 *Wright's Directory, 1900, p. 85 and Kelly's Directory of Leicestershire and Rutland, 1941, p. 98. It should be noted, however, that the increased population in 1941 was influenced by boundary changes. In 1931 the population stood at about 16,030*

7 *Richard Gurnham, 200 years. The Hosiery Unions. 1776-1996, Leicester, 1976, p. 103*

8 *National Union of Hosiery Workers. Annual Conference 1961, p. 5. These figures do not include warehousemen, menders and trimmers who had unions of their own*

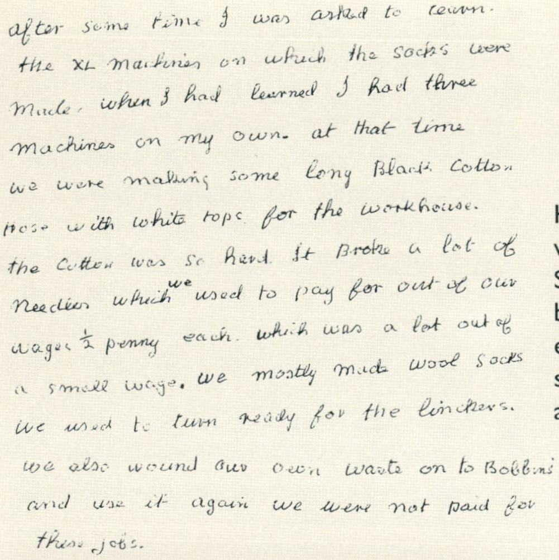
after some time I was asked to learn. the XL machines on which the socks were made. when I had learned I had three machines on my own. at that time we were making some long Black Cotton hose with white tops for the workhouse. the Cotton was so hard. It Broke a lot of Needles which we used to pay for out of our wages ½ penny each. which was a lot out of a small wage. we mostly made wool socks we used to turn ready for the linckers. we also wound our own waste on to Bobbins and use it again we were not paid for these jobs.

This lady worked as a knitter until her retirement in 1977

were once a common sight in the factory. As discussed by Marilyn Palmer "Factory production brought about a radical change in the nature of the work force employed in the hosiery industry. Power driven machines did not need the application of human muscle and so could be looked after by women rather than men". (9) A number of female respondents have talked about their jobs as knitters referring to themselves as *"makers"*. Miss Coley worked on S&G's:

> *"They made the socks, but not the tops, just the socks, you see...sometimes we had some good yarn and that was really beneficial because it was beneficial to the machine let alone to the operator. Because when we had a good yarn there was no danger, well little danger of the yarn splitting because if it split, well then, it made a smash-up on the machine and broke the needles and made waste and they didn't like waste...".*

However, the majority of women worked in the more traditional jobs. Splicing was usually work carried out by young girls and the following extract conveys the feelings of twin sisters who began their working lives as splicers:

> *"Well I left school when I was fourteen and I had no choice - my mum had already got us a job at Toon's Hosiery factory. I remember she put a little pinny on us - pair of scissors and off we went. And it was a very big factory and we were very shy. But anyway we sat on these little wooden stools all day and Mrs Coley learnt us how to clip and she was an old lady. At the end of the day we had to have plasters on our fingers 'cause we'd got big blisters where the scissors cut into us!"*

Mrs Hutt worked as a linker: *"It was well paid I mean that's what we went into the industry for. It was well known for the money".* It must be acknowledged, though, that the piece rate system which was, and still is, the basis of payment for the shop floor worker in the hosiery industry in Hinckley does not suit everyone. Not all could cope with the speed of operation needed to achieve high wage levels and a number of respondents would be pleased to see the piece rate system abolished

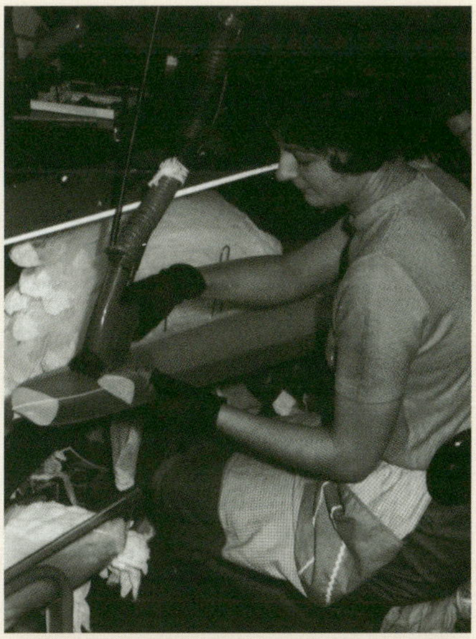

Mrs Hall working as an examiner. Mid 1960s. Note the gloves - these are worn to prevent damage to the hose (A Hall)

altogether! But as one operative states: *"When you've learnt the job you go onto piecework, then it's good money provided you work".*

A remark made by Mr Simpson also highlights the benefits for female workers in the factory system -

> *"... mechanic apprentices in the hosiery trade at that time didn't get much money...I think when I started in Atkins in 1948 I got £3.5s. a week. The young mechanic lads in the factory were not very keen on it and were leaving the job because their girlfriends could go on the linking and the overlocking and other jobs in the factory and earn far more money than the lads were earning".*

Many young women while saving to get married or setting up house preferred the financial rewards from working in the factory to the less well paid but more comfortable surroundings found in offices and shops. One respondent writes that when she left school at fifteen in 1959 she went into office work but left to work in a factory just before getting married in 1965 *"I needed more money to help with the budget".* Good money could be earned by both men and women working on the factory floor after the initial training period. But wages earned *"in the hosiery"* did and still do vary depending on the type of work undertaken. Overlocking for instance

"I graduated onto B5s making rayon stockings - 12 in a set - they used to make splicing, mock seaming and also put fashion marks on the back of the hose - about 21 fashion marks."
A shift of knitters. (Mr Maund middle back) Bennett Brothers. circa 1956. (C Maund)

9 *Palmer, Framework Knitting, p. 29*

is probably one of the highest paid female jobs while folding and bagging does not demand such high rates of pay. The pay scale generally reflects the skill attributed to the particular operation. Linking is regarded as very skilled and demands a relatively high wage and in 1962 one respondent recalls earning between £20 and £22 a week as a linker. Fully fashioned knitters could also expect high wages. This is highlighted by Mr Evans who compares his wage as a knitter with that of his father who had worked on the railways all his life:

> *"My dad weren't on a lot of money. In fact when I first went on the knitting at Hinckley at eighteen (1938) I was earning more than me father. It must have been about £5 or £6 a week. Me dad was only on £3.* And he added, *"I should say at one time in the hosiery we must have been the best paid piece workers in the Midlands".* (10)

Hosiery workers in the Midlands earned more money than their counterparts in other areas of the country and indeed in some cases wages "Were only half the Midlands levels." (11) Interestingly, however, the wages earned by hosiery workers in Lancashire, even though they were lower than those in the Midlands, were still above those "rates obtained in any alternative employment". (12)

Other respondents have compared their wages to those of relatives working in offices and other industries. For instance, Mrs Taylor came into Hinckley to work from Nuneaton in 1950 at the age of fifteen and earned about £8 a week while her sister earned £1.17s.6d working in an office. Similarly, her father, a miner, earned between £12 and £14 a week as a face worker in 1953, while her husband, working as a fully fashioned knitter, was earning £21 a week. As discussed with a factory manager, *"Years ago people came into the hosiery industry because they could earn good money - a new car, a new house - you were the tops, the cream"*. A Commemorative Handbook published in celebration of the Festival of Britain in1951 describes Hinckley as 'Stockingopolis' and states:

> "In the circular hose section of the stocking trade there are about 12,000 machines in use in Hinckley and district, out of some 23,000 in the whole of the country. Since the recent war more interest has been taken in the production of fully-fashioned stockings and whereas before the war only about six firms were making this type of hose there are now over twenty-four firms in production...." (13)

Interestingly, respondents have often recalled their first week's wage and Mr Lawrance who started work in Bradbury's in 1929 remembers *"I started on 2 1/2d an hour - a 48 hr week which made it 10s. a week and that included Saturday mornings"*. The excitement of receiving a first wage is still vivid in the memory as described by twin sisters who earned 12s. a week:

> *"We were that excited. We ran into the room where me mother worked on the welting and gave her this money. Oh we were thrilled up and she gave it to us back, our first week's wages".*

Mrs Abbot, who started work in 1966 on packing, earned £4.17s.6d in her first week *"And it was like...phew - you know. I bought my mum an iron with that!"*. It was normal practice to be paid a specified rate while training, referred to as *"bosses time or time rate"* by respondents. Once a girl had learnt her job and picked up speed she would then be put on piece rate. As explained by Mrs Berridge who started work in August 1959 as a marvel mender *"I earned 25s.* (first week's wage). *The second week I got 29s. and they put me on my own time"*.

A counterman's contribution card 1946
(K. Lockton)

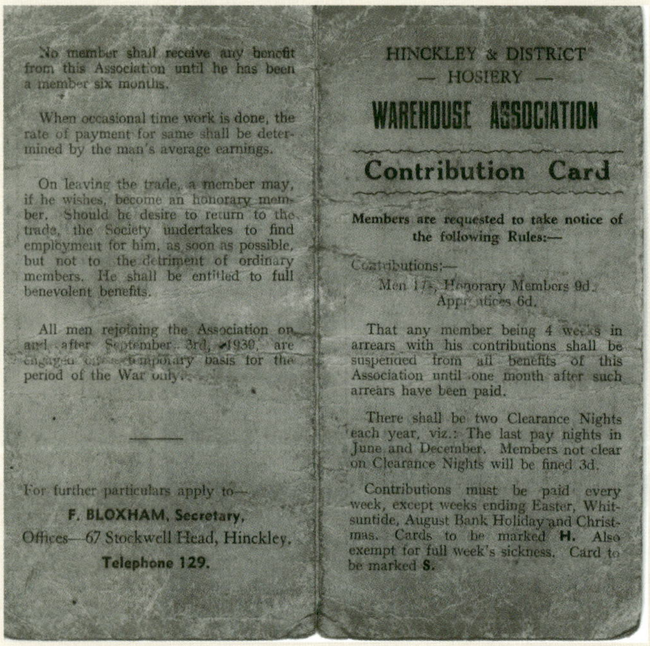

No member shall receive any benefit from this Association until he has been a member six months.

When occasional time work is done, the rate of payment for same shall be determined by the man's average earnings.

On leaving the trade, a member may, if he wishes, become an honorary member. Should he desire to return to the trade, the Society undertakes to find employment for him, as soon as possible, but not to the detriment of ordinary members. He shall be entitled to full benevolent benefits.

All men rejoining the Association on and after September 3rd, 1939, are engaged on a temporary basis for the period of the War only.

For further particulars apply to—
F. BLOXHAM, Secretary,
Offices—67 Stockwell Head, Hinckley.
Telephone 129.

HINCKLEY & DISTRICT
— HOSIERY —
WAREHOUSE ASSOCIATION

Contribution Card

Members are requested to take notice of the following Rules:—

Contributions:—
Men 1/-, Honorary Members 9d.
Apprentices 6d.

That any member being 4 weeks in arrears with his contributions shall be suspended from all benefits of this Association until one month after such arrears have been paid.

There shall be two Clearance Nights each year, viz.: The last pay nights in June and December. Members not clear on Clearance Nights will be fined 3d.

Contributions must be paid every week, except weeks ending Easter, Whitsuntide, August Bank Holiday and Christmas. Cards to be marked **H.** Also exempt for full week's sickness. Card to be marked **S.**

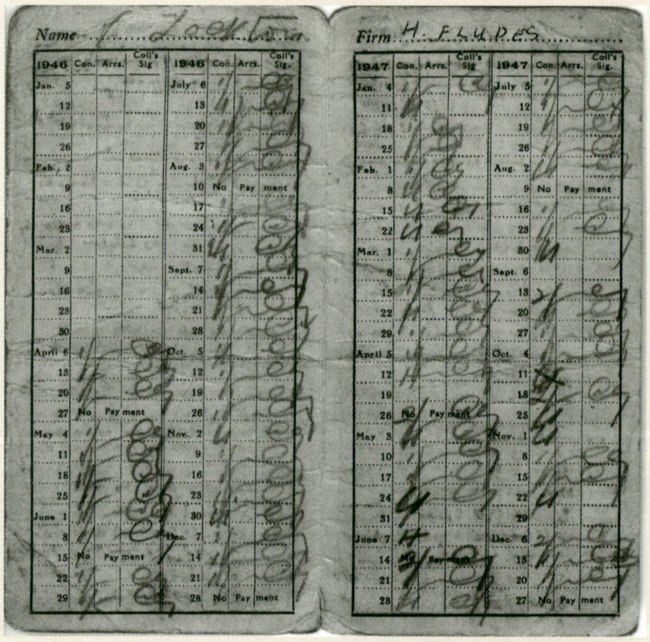

10 *Wage agreements for 1933: Interlock knitters could expect to earn between £4 and £5 a week. A fine-gauge knitter at least £5. The highest paid workers in both the lace and boot and shoe industries rarely earned more than 85s. per week See Gurnham, The Hosiery Unions p. 109*

11 *A survey carried out in 1938 found that 'Few men earned more than £3 per week in Lancashire. Men in the Midlands were earning between £3 and £5 per week. Few women were found to take home more than 32s. In the Midlands the average wage for a woman over 18 was 35s. Some could expect to earn up to £3 per week. See Gurnham, The Hosiery Unions, p. 112*

12 *ibid, p. 114*

13 *Festival of Britain, Hinckley Commemorative Handbook, p. 22, 1951*

Warehouse. Moore and Osborne. Late 1920s. (J Lloyd)
"A counterman would never get his hands dirty. He would work in a collar and tie". (J Cobley)

Innovation and dynamism, which have been characteristics of the industry since its birth, are crucial to its survival and a number of Managing Directors and other top management have stressed the need to find '*a niche in the market*' because of the intense competition. The hosiery and knitwear industry, throughout its history, but especially during the twentieth century, has also recognised the constant need to keep abreast of changes in fashion. During the inter war years rayon replaced cotton as the staple of the town and indeed Hinckley became "one of the leading growth areas (of seamless rayon hose)." (14)

During the First and Second World Wars, Hinckley, like every other manufacturing town in the country concentrated on production for the armed forces. During the 1914-1918 war, amongst other garments, Hinckley produced 3,858,797 undervests, 11,797,479 woollen drawers, 4,990,123 cardigans and jumpers, and 36,033,523 pairs of worsted socks for the armed forces (15). During the Second World War factory production became centred in a reduced number of factories, some factories having closed down, others having been requisitioned for munitions work. During this period there was an acute shortage of labour owing to workers being conscripted into the forces and into munitions but, nevertheless, during the course of the war "Millions of pairs of half-hose, huge quantities of underwear, and such things as special jerseys for jungle warfare were supplied to the Forces." (16)

The introduction of new fabrics together with changes in style of hose and knitwear, and the need to remain competitive, has necessitated adaptation, improvement and development of new machinery such as the Santoni SM8.8, Stoll, Detexomat, the Takatori, the Rosso, the Esox - these a just a few of the machines used by operatives at the present time. This need for investment in modern machinery over the years has resulted in a decrease in the number of operatives required and this is reflected in comments made by many respondents such as discussed by a former counterman who started work in 1946 at Nicholls and Wileman:

".......I went down to the Turn Stitch Turn Department. The work came off the knitting machine and this machine it turned it (stockings) on the wrong side, closed the toe and then turned it back again by suction. I mean, given at this time we had twenty female Turn Stitch Turn operators and when these new Detexomat machines came in they were either made redundant or we found them other jobs within the factory. Because this work it goes through that quickly, one Detexomat machine, I should think, does the work of about four operators".

Examining underskirts. Women in foreground examining lace which was then re-wound. The Argee, 1950s (J. Lawrance)

14 Gurnham, The Hosiery Unions, p. 103
15 Evelyn Henderson, Milestones of Hinckley 1640-1981, Hinckley, 1981, p. 12
16 Festival of Britain. Hinckley Commemorative Handbook, 1951, p. 22

Mrs. Hutt working a 22 point linking machine linking a 200 needle sock (H J Hall & Son)

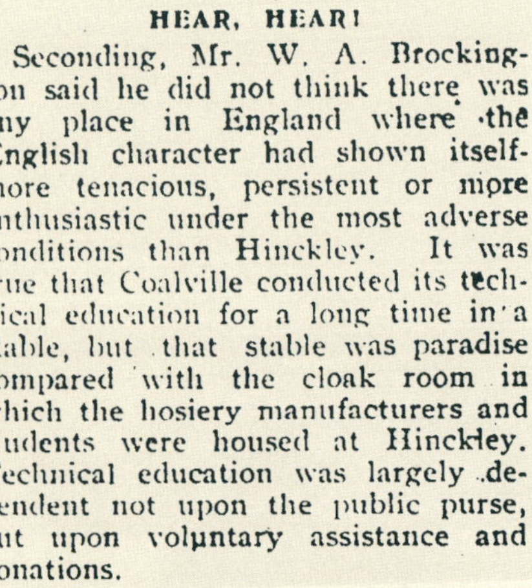

HEAR, HEAR!

Seconding, Mr. W. A. Brockington said he did not think there was any place in England where the English character had shown itself more tenacious, persistent or more enthusiastic under the most adverse conditions than Hinckley. It was true that Coalville conducted its technical education for a long time in a stable, but that stable was paradise compared with the cloak room in which the hosiery manufacturers and students were housed at Hinckley. Technical education was largely dependent not upon the public purse, but upon voluntary assistance and donations.

An extract taken from a local newspaper concerning the opening of Hinckley and District Technical College (Hinckley Times and Guardian 2/10/1931)

Miss Smart who worked in the industry for forty-six years without a break discusses the variety of jobs she did owing to changes in fashion. She started her working life at Ridley, Spriggs and Johnson in 1944 but spent most of her working life at Flude Hosiery -

> *"...well I stayed there for about two years approximately and then the machines advanced and they cut out...they were cutting out side- linking and making round heels so I thought at the time 'Well if they are cutting side-linking out they'll gradually in time cut out toe-linking' and I thought, 'They'll never cut out fully fashioned seaming, there'll always be fully-fashioned stockings' - foolish!. And I worked from cotton, lisle, rayon, pure silk and then gradually into nylon and through the different deniers of nylon before bulked yarn came in. Well then tights came in, when fully fashioned went out".*

She spent the last twenty-odd years of her working life as a tights overlocker.

Numerous operations, requiring a variety of skills and training, are necessary in the production of hose and knitwear and there is a corresponding variety of job descriptions some deemed to have a higher, but not clearly defined, status than others. Mr Bateman started his working life in 1933 as an apprentice counterman earning 7s.9d per week. In order to earn more money, he explains *"I went to Hood and Masons in the Trim Shop where they used to pull stockings on boards. I was known as a legger"*. He goes on to say that he considers trimmers and their young assistants *"A rougher sort of individual. They used to bet a lot and swear a lot and if you didn't behave yourself they could be a bit brutal"*. A counterman or warehouseman's work was considered more gentlemanly than that of a trimmer whose work was far more physical. But trimmers could earn high wages and, similar to the countermen, were represented by their own union.

The apprenticeship for a counterman lasted seven years but according to Mr Smith was *"a bit of a farce"*. Mr Lumley recalls his apprenticeship: *"I won't mention most of the jobs. I pretty well covered everything from cleaning the toilets out, to making the tea, running for fish and chips and I don't know what!"* However, once the apprenticeship had been completed great pride could be taken in the job. The job of a counterman was to pair stockings and a pot of cream was kept handy to ensure soft hands. Rough hands could damage stockings! During the 1960s, with the introduction of tights and the demise of stockings, the job of the counterman all but disappeared. These men either found other jobs within the hosiery industry or alternative work in the town. Others were able to secure positions in the car industry in Coventry which at this time was booming.

Mr Lawrance talks about his introduction into the industry in 1929 at the age of 14 as a trainee mechanic:

> *"I was an 'oily rag' for six grown-up mechanics....... that meant I had to do all the dirty jobs for all these chaps but they*

A shift of knitters. Nicholls and Wileman. 1997 (C. Maund)
"At one time a knitter had 10 - 12 machines, at present, depending on the type of garments being knitted, he can have up to 60 machines"

Fully Fashioned Stockings "...were only bought for special occasions" (Flude Hosiery)

taught me quite a lot. I mean it was an experience, really, that was quite invaluable even though it was not an official apprenticeship".

It was common practice among young mechanics and indeed all newcomers to the factory, both male and female, that they learnt the fundamentals of their job on the factory floor. They were taught by older, experienced hands who were able to pass down their knowledge and as explained by a young mechanic who started work in the 1980s:

"I did not go to Tech but was taught by older mechanics. All these men had in turn been taught their skills at Bentley's. All extremely skilled men with much knowledge to pass on".

However, it must be emphasised that over the years many young people have attended the local technical college as part of their apprenticeships and also to improve their skills. Many, in the process, have attained City & Guilds and more recently NVQ qualifications. A number have also gone on to do HNC or similar courses at a higher level. Many perceive jobs in the hosiery as being repetitive and boring but it must be acknowledged that certain jobs do take considerable skill and learning. Mr Smith explains the training of a fully fashioned linker in knitwear:

"A linker will probably take up to twelve months before she can get anywhere near earning a wage - that's neck linking - 16 point neck link and also we do 14 point link - it's a long training programme, especially when you got to think that you have got to build the speed up as well as quality - quality comes first, speed comes second".

It has become obvious from interviews and replies to questionnaires, that those employed in the hosiery have a deep sense of pride in their work and a depth of knowledge related to their skills. There are obvious concerns over short time working, depression in the industry, intense competition from abroad, redundancies and pay freezes. Disillusionment has been expressed with the current state of the industry but, interestingly, this is not a new phenomenon. Depression in the industry has been ever present and has affected the people of the town and district over the centuries. Following the Napoleonic Wars "fearful depression" (17) was experienced by the country as a whole and as stated by Marilyn Palmer "The framework knitting industry did not recover until the introduction of steam-powered frames in the 1870s". (18) The industry has also been very much dictated to by the "whims of fashion". For instance, from about 1810 "Men began wearing trousers, and breeches with hose ceased to be generally worn" (19). Women's fashions between about 1790 and 1820 dictated that "ladies' skirt lengths rose approximately from the ankle to slightly above and resulted in increased patterning being applied to ladies' hose" (20). The introduction of the mini skirt in the 1960s brought about the development of tights which may be said to have revolutionised the industry. These fashion changes along with the introduction of new fibres such as rayon in the early twentieth century, nylon in the late 1940s and more recently lycra have required manufacturers to keep abreast of current trends and developments. The first and second World Wars also necessitated adaptation to the war effort and resulted in changes from the production of fashion wear to more functional clothing for civilians and armed forces alike to meet government quotas.

The textile industry, then, can be seen as having to be extremely dynamic, and adaptability and innovation by those working in the industry is of the utmost importance. The following observation reflects the feelings expressed by numerous respondents and may be a fitting conclusion:

"Investment must be encouraged, after all we make better quality goods. Lets hope that in years to come the trade gets stronger. After all we in the Hinckley area have the tools and the know how to do the job".

"An open toe surgical hose being pre-boarded to shape" (M. Smith) (Scholl Consumer Products)

17 Pickering, The Cradle and Home of the Hosiery Traade, p. 47
18 Palmer, Framework Knitting, p. 18
19 John Millington & Stanley Chapman, Four Centuries of Machine Knitting, England, 1989, p. 29
20 ibid, p. 29

Social Life in the Factory

"We Had Lots of Fun in Them Days"

Documented information contained in inventories, wills, indenture certificates, parish records, census returns, newspaper articles and the like provide factual records of peoples lives. Similarly, information on the types of machinery, production rates, union agitation and wages can be recovered from a variety of government sources and books. Social historians have traditionally relied on such sources to piece together a picture of the working conditions, the state of trade and numbers involved in industries at any given time. But what do we know about the social lives of those who worked and still work in the factory? By talking to people one learns not only about the stresses and strains of daily factory life but also about the good times, the laughter and the jesting, the social interaction and camaraderie which are fundamental aspects in the day-to-day lives in a factory environment. As stated by David Hey "Oral history can create intimate portraits of people, places and communities in a way that other historical methods can't; and it allows the lives of ordinary people.......and of groups who are underrepresented in the records of the community to be given their proper place in the overall scheme of things"(1). The following is based on extracts from written accounts and recorded discussions with people in the hosiery trade in the Hinckley area and brings alive the day to day social life of factory workers in a town heavily reliant on the textile trade for its economic welfare.

Factory work over the years has necessitated both day and night shift working: night work traditionally being the province of the male knitters while day work saw a great influx of employees to the factory floor. During the inter-war years daytime factory hours were long, *"8 o'clock till 1 o'clock, an hour for dinner, then 2 till 6 o'clock. And, of course, Saturday mornings 8 till 11 o'clock, which made a total of forty-eight hours a week"*. A number of respondents have recalled family members pre 1914 who worked a twelve hour day: 6 o'clock in the morning until 6 o'clock in the evening and three hours on a Saturday. Over the years working hours have reduced, flexi-time has been introduced in many factories and Saturday morning work is now a rarity rather than the norm. Mrs Judd, who started work in the late 1960s, recalls that:

> *"In the early years the time you had to work were from 8 o'clock in the morning to 5 o'clock in the evening but after about six years they brought in the flexi-time and I used to be at work for just gone 7 o'clock in the morning and work until 5 o'clock or half-past five in the evening and then would finish at about 11 o'clock on a Friday morning".*

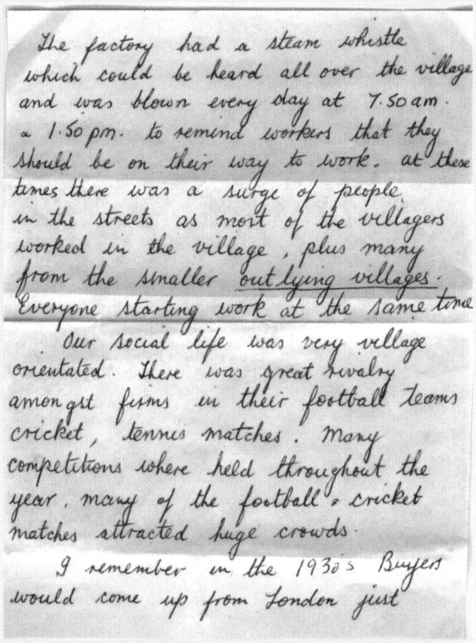
The factory had a steam whistle which could be heard all over the village and was blown every day at 7.50am. & 1.50pm. to remind workers that they should be on their way to work. at these times there was a surge of people in the streets as most of the villagers worked in the village, plus many from the smaller outlying villages. Everyone starting work at the same time

Our social life was very village orientated. There was great rivalry amongst firms in their football teams cricket, tennis matches. Many competitions where held throughout the year, many of the football & cricket matches attracted huge crowds.

I remember in the 1930's Buyers would come up from London just

Mr. Lumley began his working life in 1928 at the age of 14 and followed in the footsteps of his Uncle Tom. (B. Lumley)

Factory operatives arriving for work by bus and cycle (Hinckley Library Local Studies Collection)

---

1 *Stephen Caunce, Oral History and the Local Historian, (From the editorial by David Hey) London, 1994*

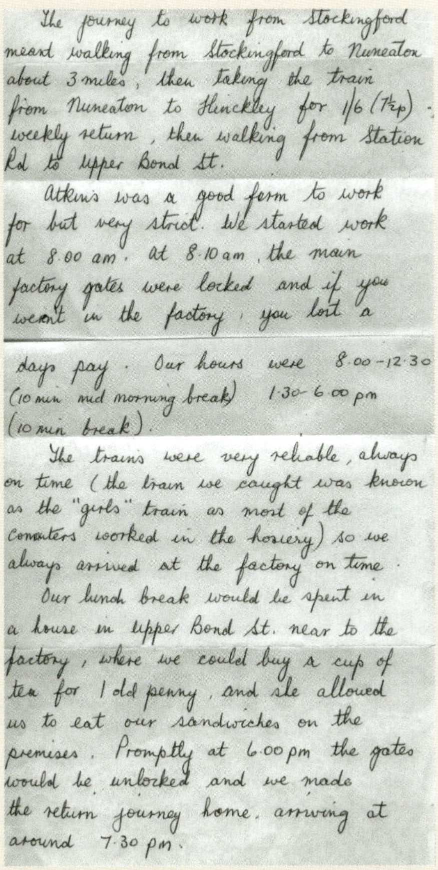
The journey to work from Stockingford meant walking from Stockingford to Nuneaton about 3 miles, then taking the train from Nuneaton to Hinckley for 1/6 (7½p) weekly return, then walking from Station Rd to Upper Bond St.

Atkins was a good firm to work for but very strict. We started work at 8.00 am. At 8.10 am, the main factory gates were locked and if you weren't in the factory, you lost a days pay. Our hours were 8.00-12.30 (10 min mid morning break) 1.30-6.00 pm (10 min break).

The trains were very reliable, always on time (the train we caught was known as the "girls" train as most of the commuters worked in the hosiery) so we always arrived at the factory on time.

Our lunch break would be spent in a house in Upper Bond St. near to the factory, where we could buy a cup of tea for 1 old penny, and she allowed us to eat our sandwiches on the premises. Promptly at 6.00 pm the gates would be unlocked and we made the return journey home, arriving at around 7.30 pm.

"It was through my sisters connections that I started work at Atkins in 1932 earning 7/6 a week sticking tabs on stockings which were made of lisle, artificial silk and pure silk"
D. Lumley

Miss Coley, who was born in 1904, remembers as a young girl delivering breakfast to members of her family who worked at Hurst Cottons in Earl Shilton. She used a short cut through the fields to the factory and vividly recalls taking pains to avoid a bull kept in one of the pastures. This was one of her family chores before going to school:

> *"My mother used to send me down there with the breakfasts for three of them. Sometimes they used to have eggs...bacon and eggs, you know, like in sandwiches, you see. Yes I used to carry this can of tea. Their breakfast was eight until half-past."*

Up until the 1960s those working within cycling or walking distance of their place of work went home for their dinner. A full cooked meal would be served up. Mrs Pegg, who lived very close to the place where both her and her husband worked, recalls the preparation of hot meals:

> *"Well, when we were first married we worked at Toons. I used to nip out about 11o'clock in the morning and put it on low and it would be nearly done when you got home. My mum used to do that, as well, when she worked there."*

Those who came from further afield, however, had to make alternative arrangements and Mrs Maund's mother who came from Sapcote to work in Earl Shilton used to pay to eat with a family in the village.

During the industry's heyday and before the car became the dominant mode of transport, people from outlying villages came to work on buses, trains and bikes. Many respondents remember when Hinckley, Earl Shilton and Barwell were *"chock-a-block"* with buses and cycles first thing in the morning and early evening bringing people to work from outlying villages and taking them home again. One respondent now in her nineties remembers a friend who used to cycle to work from Ibstock to Earl Shilton, a distance of around ten miles and that-

> *"...some used to come from Newbold and others Barlestone - there used to be coach loads. But some, you know, just came on their bicycles. And then they had to stand up all day because they worked S&G's".*

The majority of workers travelling to Hinckley from surrounding areas were women and girls, *"the hosiery"* acting as a magnet for large numbers of female workers for the shop floor. It was quite normal for women to carry on working after marriage, unlike some female employment of the day where a marriage bar existed (2). Indeed, hosiery employers encouraged women who wished to carry on working after marriage, and in some cases after having children, as it helped to foster a family feeling within the workplace and dependable labour was not lost to the industry. Most women continued working out of necessity and as highlighted by one respondent who was born in 1932 and placed with a childminder at six weeks old: *"My dad was never well and my mum went back to work"*. Those women who gave up factory work after having a child would often take in outwork, thus helping to supplement the family income until children were old enough to *"fend for*

Cricket Team, H Flude & Co. Mr Harry Flude, Chairman and founder member of the business is seated in the centre.
(Flude Hosiery)

2 *Jose Castle discusses the marraige bar which was enforced at Courtaulds in 'Factory Work for Women: Courtaulds & GEC between the Wars' in Bill Lancaster and Tony Morris, Life and Labour in the Twentieth Century City. The Experience of Coventry, Coventry, 1986, p. 133-171. Shani D'Cruze also discusses the subject: "The marraige bar admitted unmarried women into, but excluded married women from the professional and white collar workforce" in 'Women and the family' in June Purvis, An Introduction. Women's History: Britain, 1850 - 1945, 1995, p. 74*

themselves". The women would then frequently return to the factory floor. The hosiery industry is still heavily reliant on its network of female outworkers who, for whatever reason, prefer to work from home.

Even those respondents who have spoken negatively about "*bosses*" and the industry as a whole have, nevertheless, felt an empathy with their employer. In many instances they considered their employer to be a hard working man with a sense of responsibility for his work force. Many an employer had built up the business from relatively humble beginnings with a set of knitting machines in a small workshop and the boss would often be known personally by his workers and vice versa. They would attend the same services in the local church or chapel, go to the same pubs and play the same sports. Sport in fact was an important pastime for the men working in the factories. Inter-factory football matches, darts, dominoes and cricket fostered a social link between employees in different factories. Mr Lumley recollects that during the 1930s Mr Bradbury (a manufacturer) "*Had got a football cup which he donated to the factories to be played competitively for charity. And it was called the Sunshine Cup*".

Many interesting and entertaining anecdotes have been related about the interaction between the workers and the boss. Applying for a pay rise was an "*art in itself*" and Mr Lawrance (who worked for A H Bradbury in Earl Shilton at this time) was careful to choose the right moment: "*I were friendly with the warehouse manager who used to go down to the office to do the post and he'd give me the nod to tell me that the boss was in a good mood to apply for a rise*". Many employees have commented on the "*tightness*" of their employer when it came to wages and one young girl who started work in 1917 was summoned to the factory office because she had earned the princely sum of £3.9s in one week working on piece rate:

> "*....the boss were there, his son were there and the manager were there. And they asked me how old I were and they said 'Don't you think that's a lot of money for a girl your age?'. And they settled to give me a regular wage of £2.15s. a week*".

Some manufacturers were "*tyrants*" as far as time keeping was concerned and a number of respondents have spoken about bosses waiting at the factory gates for late comers. Others have spoken of money being docked from their wages for arriving just after clocking-on time of 8 o'clock. Mr Cobley remembers his first boss, Perc Beasley, and how the young lads were frightened of him, because he was so strict and "*woe betide poor timekeepers!*"

> "*...he was there first thing in the morning and he was there last thing at night. He was very, very strict. He used to go work early, say, 6 o'clock in the morning. Now we didn't used to start work till 8 o'clock but if you wasn't there before 8 o'clock he'd be gone home for his breakfast and you had to stand outside till he came back!*"

Studio Photo of Ada Harrison and friends on holidays in Great Yarmouth 1925. Note the fashionable clothes worn by the group of friends. Factory floor workers organised their own savings club, sometimes called the "Didlum Club", whereby workers could save so much each week towards the their annual weekly holiday. (M.Maud)

Factory outing to Blackpool "And a good time was had by all" (Flude Hosiery)

Mr Haywood as a young apprentice remembers how he and his fellow apprentices would deliver outwork to women living in Earl Shilton, Barwell and Elmesthorpe and they would be given bottles of pop, bags of sweets and sometimes a cigarette by the women. These young lads started work at fourteen and it would seem that whenever they could they would be off playing football, having a furtive cigarette or even taking apples from the boss's fruit tree -

> "*...at the back of the factory was quite a few fruit trees which belonged to Mr Wileman and we were not allowed to touch them. At one point in time one of my so called friends said to me 'You go up the tree and throw the apples down.' So I was up the tree throwing these apples down when a voice said to me 'Are those apples yours?' And I looked down and there was Mr Wileman himself...*".

On another occasion Mr Haywood recalls that he and his "*comrades*" were sent home for playing football in the factory cellar *"And the manager told us we could come back in the morning and see 'if you've still got a job!"*.

Some of the manufacturers seem to have exhibited a degree of eccentricity and one manufacturer, Mr Carey Toon, was known to dislike toe stitching much preferring the better finish which was produced on a linking machine. As explained by Mrs Pegg;

> *"You'd find your machine had been taken out when you'd got there the next morning. You didn't know what you were going to do. You'd end up doing any old job..... backwinding or cutting up waste something like that...!"*.

However, Mrs Pegg also recalls Mr Toon having a generous side and that in 1950 he held a party at the Working Men's Club in Earl Shilton to celebrate the one hundredth anniversary of the family business. A wonderful time was had by all: free drink and food, music and dancing! Indeed dances were an annual event in many factories and looked forward to by both employer and employee. Very often the George Hotel, Hinckley would be hired for the night and entertainers such as Harry Roy, Ivy Benson and Jack Parnell were engaged for the evening. A number of companies in the local area organised an annual outing, often to the seaside: Blackpool, Rhyl, Skegness were amongst the resorts visited and many fond memories have been related of a day out on the company. Mr Dixon, in particular, remembers a trip to London "*... all these women who I worked with on a day-to-day basis in the factory... when I saw them dolled up, I mean, they were gorgeous!*".

The factory system of production fostered a close working community not least because of the proximity of the various machines and benches. As described by Mrs Hutt who worked at a number of factories during the 1950s:

Rough mending before stockings were taken to be dyed *"The knitting and every finishing operation is carefully examined by expert girls..."* Nicholls & Wileman (P. Haywood)

> *"We were like sardines in a tin. Not much room, they packed so many people in at that time. It were good fun, you could have a talk, have a laugh"*.

Mrs Kind highlights the friendliness and social interaction felt between workmates on the factory floor and recalls:

> *"It was hard work but ...of course we were picture mad then, you know, with Robert Taylor and all them and all over the wall there would be photos of film stars and everybody would be saying 'Have you been to pictures, have you seen this....' We'd hear...oh - who had been dancing and things. It used to be great"*.

Mrs Lee who started work in the mid 1950s also remembers the friendliness which extended into out-of-work activities:

> *"In the old days we'd go to work with our rollers in. Tie head scarves round our rollers and come home-time, switch machine off and dash up to the toilet and do your hair, you know. I used to do this other girl's hair. She wasn't very good at it - back-combing . We used to do all that. Straight after we'd finished work - off out to the pictures or wherever"*.

Centenary Celebration Luncheon 1950, J Toon & Sons "A Smashing Do" (Mr & Mrs Pegg)

It must be acknowledged, however, that there was friction, frequently because earnings were based on piece rate. At times there were complaints that "*so-and-so*" was getting the best work leaving the more difficult and less productive work to others. There were also complaints against the mechanics because while a machine stood idle no money was being earned. For this reason many operatives including knitters and overlockers learned to repair their own machines. In the winter the factory was often reported as too cold, in the summer it was too hot. There were complaints about noise levels and operatives became proficient at "*lip reading*"; there were complaints about windows being left open causing draughts; complaints about the "*foremisses*" or the foreman being too strict or not strict enough and as recalled by Mrs Hall

> *"I thought the foreman was lovely but he was such a weak, weak man. He let all these Nuneaton girls...they'd go for cigarettes, you know and they'd stand talking for ages".*

A number of respondents have also commented on the bad language used especially when a knitting machine went wrong:

> *"There'd be a big smash-up (on the XLs) and this man he put his hands on his hips and he'd say all the bad words he could think of to this machine".*

Mrs Turton remembers when she first started work at fifteen, in the late 1960s at T Jennings and Son, no-one spoke to her, everyone was in their "*own little clique*" and if you worked too hard you'd be called a "*scrat*".

Disagreements, quarrels and bad feeling between employees have been mentioned by respondents but such discord was more often than not sorted out by friends acting as mediators or in some cases by the local union representative. As explained by Mrs Godfrey "*You made life-long friendships. We still mix socially with the people we worked with years ago*". People have also spoken about factory floor romances which often blossomed into life long partnerships. Factory life and social life often merged, as friends in the factory met in the evenings and weekends to go to the pictures, dancing and on the *"Monkey run"*.

Teasing and playing jokes on fellow workers or your boss was indulged in whenever possible, especially by the young people. Mrs Hall remembers-

> *"...they put me in the works trolley and sent me through into the makers room - deserted me - and I was stuck in this trolley amongst all these makers..."*

As described by Mrs Grouse talking about a friend whose "*high-jinx*" went a bit far with the foreman's hat at Toon's factory-

> *"...he always used to wear these hard bowler hats and well you know what you're like when you're sixteen, you're lairy aren't you? Well she put his hat on - this bowler hat and she started dancing round the room and she pulled it and the whole brim came right off. Oh he were angry he were..."*

Mr Bateman remembers that while working the night shift as a knitter at John Gents, he and his mates played a couple of tricks on an older colleague whose pride and joy was a BSA motor bike:

> *"One night we decided to pinch his bike and tie it up to the hot water pipes. Another time we took his bike home and didn't tell him where it had gone and he had to walk home. When he got home his wife said to him 'What did you send your bike home for...'?"*

The plaques on either side of the girl reads:

Hinckley is justly proud of its hosiery tradition. One of the earliest centres to manufacture hosiery. It still preserves the spirit of progress and jealously guards its position as the centre of a great industry.
Its workers are the children of earlier craftsmen, and though time has brought many and diverse changes, are recognised as the most efficient operatives in the hosiery trade in modern times.

Jubilee Parade 1935 in honour of George V's 25 years reign as King
(Hinckley & District Knitting Industry Association)

Beauty Competitions were also held at various venues in the town - the George Hotel being a favourite place for social events. Miss Lovely Legs Competitors - circa 1947 (Flude Hosiery)

Retirement and 60th Birthday celebration. Fludes circa 1989 (M.Smart)

Singing while working was a frequent pastime and enjoyed by many over the years even though the factory "buzzed" with the working of machinery. Miss Coley recalls:

> *"There was about six of us working together and we used to sing a lot and this singing it were dreadful. We all used to sing a different song and all begin together. It was a horrible noise!".*

However, Mr Lawrance remembers more harmonious renderings. He recalls that during the war years employees at Halls in Stoke Golding would strike up a hymn -

> *"...and everybody would join in and we got such a quality of singers in the factory that it was like a real choir. One of the favourites was the sixty-fifth Psalm and where it comes to 'Where little hills rejoice' all the men were banging and thumping".*

Mr Lawrance felt that the singing made life more pleasant and tolerable during the hardships experienced as a result of blackouts and rationing which affected both the working and domestic lives of people.

"Workers Playtime", "Music While You Work" and "Housewives Choice" were wireless shows listened to avidly by employees on the factory floor. Mrs Judd recalls that while working as an overlocker at the Argee they were allowed to play records "*...in an afternoon - Elvis, Gene Pitney, Bobby Vee - and if you and your friend liked the same record you used to wave to each other. It seems a very strange thing to do but that's what we did!*" Today the use of personal stereos has replaced the wireless although the radio can still be heard in the background.

The working week then was not just one long grind. It would appear that those who worked and still work in the industry had and have a great capacity to enjoy themselves in what many may perceive as boring, repetitive and monotonous work. Friday treats, birthdays, dressing-up brides and grooms, days out, Christmas parties, dances, retirement celebrations are amongst the activities which people have spoken about. Many of the activities participated in during working hours may be regarded as traditional. Take for instance Friday treats, an activity which perhaps started soon after factories became established in the local area, and have been spoken about as an opportunity for employees to indulge themselves at the end of a working week. A bag of sweets shared amongst work mates, "*a luscious cake*" or as in the case of Mrs Pegg who started her working life in the early 1940s at Toons, a far more elaborate treat, "*Oh yes! On Fridays we always used to take fruit and cream in and have cream cakes, cups of tea and it always lasted longer than it should have*". Mr Dixon, working as a factory manager in the late 1950s, remembers sitting down with a small group of women

> *"And round about 3 o'clock on a Friday afternoon I used to go round to Mrs P and her mates - four of them and me - would just have a little port and brandy just to set the weekend off".*

Dressing up brides-to-be and grooms-to-be is also an activity which has been around for many years, these young people often being tied to lamp posts in a prominent position for all to see. Mr Startin remembers being dressed as a fairy "*...a seventeen stone rugby prop. They* *took all me clothes off me. I had to motor bike all the way home to Stoney Stanton!"* At Nicholls and Wileman in Earl Shilton Mrs Grouse recalls that the bride-to-be would bring wine and cake for everyone and -

> *"...we used to make them a lovely big hat and make paper roses and put her a long dress on and she'd go all round the factory giving everybody cake and a drink. And it used to be really nice. I can remember once, the groom also worked at the factory so they were both there. And that day they went a bit far really - they put them in one of these big trolleys what you shove the work in. And we took them outside and over the zebra crossing and to the Co-op and tied them up so they couldn't get out. We had lots of fun...lots of fun in them days".*

A male respondent who was married in the early 1970s recalls having to take the jesting in good spirit:

> *"...they took me coat out from where it was hung - sewed the bottoms of me sleeves up, piled talcum powder and confetti in there, and I had to wear that. They painted your face up as well - lipstick and all that. Traipsed you all round the different departments, looking like a clown. It was all in good fun, you know. Then they would give you the present, from the boss as well".*

Nostalgically Mr Smith declares that:

> *"Those are what you might call the good old days - things changed over the years - they still do dressing up when you're getting married but not the fun and games we used to have in the good old days".*

The majority of respondents have spoken about the changes which took place during the late 1960s and 1970s and that there was no longer *"time to sit and talk"*. As explained by Mrs Read who worked in the industry all her life and retired in the early 1990s:

> *"You know, you never went work worrying. Like everybody says today that they are stressed out with the jobs, you weren't stressed out years ago... in the last ten years of your working life you used to come home literally drained, but in the years before you didn't. Like I say everybody were nice..."*

The phrase "*rat race*" begins to crop up in the conversations. Community spirit and friendliness between colleagues which people spoke about in the earlier years gives way to a more insular attitude. It is difficult to wholly attribute this sense of loss to respondents viewing the past through 'rose tinted glasses'. During the mid 1960s and the 1970s a vast amount of government legislation was introduced bringing about changes in working practices: Industrial Training Boards, The Redundancy Payment Act, The Protection of Employment Act, Equal Pay, Sex Discrimination and Health and Safety Legislation, all had an effect on the industry. Cheap imports and the oil crises of the early 1970s had a serious impact on the home market. These factors significantly influenced working life and conditions in the factories.

Workers' days out on the firm, which had fostered a sense of camaraderie and goodwill, were gradually phased out and replaced by longer holiday entitlement for the individual. Christmas parties in the factory were memorable occasions but legislation now forbids alcohol on the shop floor. Festive celebrations do still take place with the boss joining in: One manufacturer is recorded to have dressed up as Wee Willy Winkie at a Christmas *"do"* in the not so distant past! Mr Simpson recalls a typical Christmas *"do"* in the early 1950s when he used to work -

> *"...with the ladies on the old George machines, it was lovely, they used to bring cakes in and bottles of wine and have a sing-song and people would end up in the Barley Sheaf and the Liberal Club. Oh yes! quite a lot of factory romances in those days".*

Though much of the legislation and change has proved beneficial this appears to have resulted in a loss of closeness in the people. Life on the factory floor may be perceived as a reflection of society in general and respondents have commented on the pace of life and the stress that is ever present in work and outside the working environment. As discussed by Mr Smith who sums up the general feelings of many of those interviewed:

> *"Things have changed all round - some for the best, some not for the best. The girls on the shop floor have got better conditions - far better conditions. The work space itself, whereas in the old days you were walking around falling over the work all over the place, now the environment is clear. You've got the work by the machines and you've got health and safety rules and you have got to adhere to them. It's a rat race, though, it is definitely a rat race".*

Lynne and John were married in 1976
(J. Chinn)

"Celebrating the festive season"
Iway Hosiery, Burbage, 1970s
(M. Smart)
"Well you always decorated-up for Christmas, you know, you always put trimmings up .... and we used to have some lovely Christmas parties"
(Mrs Read)

Conclusion

For generations, Hinckley people in their thousands have been employed in the hosiery and knitting trade. By the end of the twentieth century, whilst still a major employer in the area, fewer people now work in the industry than in the recent past. Many former factories have closed down and others have reduced the size of their workforce. Although the hosiery and knitwear industry has been hard hit by world wide economic recession and has also been adversely affected by the global marketplace, it nevertheless continues to adapt and change to current and future methods of production, incorporating new technologies and more automation in manufacturing techniques. As well as being a modern, forward-looking industry using the latest in computer technology, there is still a large demand for the more traditional skills of both male and female workers. Many Hinckley firms have been able to find a market niche, specialising in making particular products of quality, often with a much shorter time from order to completion than overseas competitors.

More opportunities for employment in other industries locally are available because of economic diversification. Hinckley's young people no longer grow up and leave school with the automatic expectation of working in a hosiery factory. Even so, the hosiery trade is still important to all the area's inhabitants. Almost everyone, even if they are not involved with the industry themselves, will know someone working in the trade or will have family members from earlier generations who did. Many institutions vital to the well-being of the community, such as the hospital, library and college of further education, owe their initial existence to the wealth generated in the industry or to the community spirit of those who worked in it.

This book has attempted to trace the story of the people who, over the last 350 years, have contributed to the growth of the town's staple industry into world wide significance and have thereby helped shape the town. From the earliest introduction and adoption in the locality of framework knitting, through the domestic stage of the industry, moving through frameshops and into the factory age, the town and its main industry from the point of view of the people involved in it has been investigated. This is not intended to be a definitive history. For those wanting to learn the story of Hinckley from a broader perspective the earlier books by A J Pickering, H J Francis and Hugh Beavin are excellent. It has been the purpose of this publication to present new information or existing knowledge in a different way in order to show how anyone can be involved in making history.

The story does not end here. It is up to you to tell the next stage of the story. Think about your own working life or that of other family members and friends. How long have you or your family lived in the area? If you are recent arrivals, why did you come here? At work, what things are or were significant? What is or was enjoyable about it? If you can record or write down your experiences then you are creating an historical record for future generations to learn from and add to.

Despite its lack of any particularly grand or spectacular buildings, although there are some gems for those who care to look, the real heritage of Hinckley and its nearby villages and its investment in and contribution to the future is its people.

Further Reading

Bibliography

G Bowles & S Kirrane,
Knitting Together - Memories of Leicestershire's Hosiery Industry, Leicester, 1990

Cynthia Brown,
Wharf Street Remembered, Leicester Living History Unit, 1997

Richard Candee,
Domestic Industry in the Factory Age: Anglo-American Development of the "Family" Knitting Machine, Textile History, Volume 29, Number 1, Spring 1998

Stephen Caunce,
Oral History and the Local Historian, London, 1994

Charlotte Ericson,
British Industrialists - Steel and Hosiery 1850 - 1950, Cambridge, 1959

W Felkin,
An Account of the Machine-wrought Hosiery Trade: its extent and the condition of the framework-knitters: being a paper read in the statistical section, at the second York meeting of the British Association held September 18, 1844, together with evidence given under the Hosiery Commission Inquiry,London, 1845

H J Francis,
History of Hinckley, Hinckley, 1930

R Gurnham,
200 Years - The Hosiery Unions 1776-1976, Leicester, 1976

Evelyn Henderson,
Milestones of Hinckley 1640-1981, Hinckley, 1981

E J Hobsbawm,
The Machine Breakers, Labouring Men, London, 1964

Stephen Humphries,
The Handbook of Oral History - Recording Life Stories, London, 1984

B Lancaster & T Mason,
Life and Labour in a Twentieth Century City - The Experience of Coventry, Coventry, 1986

Norman Longmate,
The Hungry Mills, London, 1978

J Millington & S Chapman,
Four Centuries of Machine Knitting, England, 1989

Lionel M Munby,
The Luddites in the Period 1779-1830, The Luddites and Other Essays, Edgware, 1971

D Nash & D Reeder,
Leicester in the Twentieth Century, Leicester, 1993

John Nichols,
History and Antiquities of Hinckley, 1782: Abridged reproduction of the 1872 edition, edited by David J Knight, for Hinckey Museum, 1993

M Palmer,
Framework Knitting, Shire Album 119, 1984

Bill Partridge,
The Daniel Payne Story, Knitting International, February, 1991

A J Pickering,
Cradle and Home of the Hosiery Trade 1640-1940, Hinckley, 1940

J Purvis,
An Introduction to Women's History: Britain, 1850-1945, London, 1995

E Roberts,
Women and Families - An Oral History, 1940-1970, Oxford, 1995

Victoria History of the Counties of England
Victoria History of Leicestershire. Vol.3

Sally Westwood,
All Day Every Day - Factory and family in the making of women's live, London, 1984

Transactions of the Leicestershire Archaelogical Society, Volume IV

Other Sources

Oral Interviews undertaken between July 1997 and December 1998
Filled in Questionnaires
Interviews with Managing Directors
Factory Visits
Discussions with local historians: Mr Hugh Beavin, Mr Bill Partridge, Mr Joe Lawrance, Rev. Peter Hewis

Newspapers:

Daily Telegraph, 22 December 1859
Hinckley Journal, 30 July, 17 August, 23 December 1859, January - December 1862
Hinckley Times, 26 May 1989 (Article entitled "The Great Strike" by Bill Partridge)
Leicester Chronicle, 18 March, 8 April 1826
London Times, 22 December 1859
First Appendix to the Report on the Condition of Framework Knitters, 1845
Hinckley Techinical College Governor's Meeting Minute Books, 1891 onwards
Hinckley Parish Magazine, November, 1873; April 1874
Hinckley and District Co-operative Society Limited, A Brief History of its Rise and Progress, 1861-1911, published as a souvenir of its fiftieth anniversary, Hinckley 1911

Privately published pamphlets:

Atkins of Hinckley 1722-1972
A Century of Hosiery Manufacture, J Toon & Sons Ltd
The Flude Story
Halls History 1882-1982
Manchester Hosiery Manufacturing Company Limited
Nicholls & Wileman Ltd.
Festival of Britain, Hinckley Commemorative Handbook 1951
Hosiery in Hinckley, Arranged by Joe Lawrance and Bill Partridge

Trade Directories:

Kelly's Directory of Leicestershire and Rutland, 1941
Melville and Company, Directory and Gazeteer, 1854
Wright's Directory, 1900
National Union of Hosiery Workers. Annual Conference 1961
Leicestershire Records Office, Wigston Magna, Leics for all other original documents and primary materials

Valuable Stoc
TO BE SOLD BY
BY MESSRS.
HARROLD
(WITHOUT RESER
On THURSDAY, the 7th day
At the BULL'S HEAD INN, MAR
THE FOLLOWING VALUAB
FRAM
Subject to such Conditions as will be th
WHERE AT.
Lot. No. Gage. Width.
WHERE A
26.—264 24 15 James Bonser's,
27.— 41 26 15 Charles Bonser's,
28.—116 24 15 Thomas Moore's
29.— 55 24 15 John Moore's,
30.—303 24 15 Charles Mould's,
31.— 64 26 15 Isaac Underwood's,
32.— 73 24 14 William Herbert's,